VIVA THE ENTREPRENEUR

FOUNDING, SCALING, *and*

RAISING VENTURE CAPITAL *in*

LATIN AMERICA

THE
ENTREPRENEUR

BRIAN REQUARTH

LIONCREST
PUBLISHING

VIVA THE ENTREPRENEUR
Founding, Scaling, and Raising Venture Capital in Latin America

ISBN   978-1-5445-0863-4 *Hardcover*

978-1-5445-0862-7 *Paperback*

978-1-5445-0861-0 *Ebook*

978-1-5445-0864-1 *Audiobook*

A special thanks to my wife, who has been my co-pilot on this journey. From English classes to raising kids, and now embarking on her own entrepreneurial endeavor.

Thanks to my parents, the best listeners in the world.

CONTENTS

FOREWORD
BY LINDA ROTTENBERG

I first met Brian Requarth in 2014, when he was already fairly well-known in the Brazilian ecosystem. Although he is American, he had built a strong reputation in Brazil and Latin America for his impact on the tech market.

Brian told me how he had been influenced by an amazing case study that had come out a few years earlier from Stanford Business School about Marcos Galperin, the co-founder—along with Hernan Kazah—of MercadoLibre.

Marcos and Hernan graduated from Stanford Business in the late nineties and could have easily gone the consulting/finance route, landing at McKinsey or Goldman Sachs. Or they could have gone to the Valley to work for one of the new firms. Instead, they did something highly unusual at the time: returned to their home country to start a company there. They took the eBay model and brought it to Latin America. Today, of course,

MercadoLibre is a juggernaut with a market cap equal to or even exceeding that of eBay (and Brazil is by far MELI's largest market). But it is quite possible that none of this would have happened if Marcos and Hernan hadn't been inspired *themselves* by the story of another legendary entrepreneur, Wences Casares.

After his company, Patagon.com, had been poised to become the E-trade of Latin America, Wences was turned down by thirty-four investors. It was a different environment back then, and people still clung to the crazy belief that the next hot startup could never come out of an emerging market like Latin America (more on that shortly). This was something that we at Endeavor were passionate about trying to change—and so we took Wences on as an Endeavor entrepreneur, helping him raise venture capital, find his first COO, and more (he even ended up marrying my assistant, Belle!). Then, lo and behold, eighteen months after he started working with us, Wences sold Patagon.com to Banco Santander for $750 million.

That was back in 1998, and it changed everything. First, all of the thirty-four investors who had rejected Wences called me and said, "Hey, do you have another kid with a crazy idea?" Then, in the months that followed, people became inspired throughout Latin America by Wences' example—*hey, if he can do it, maybe I can do it too!*—and among that group were Marcos and Hernan. Ultimately, they became Endeavor entrepreneurs too.

Flash forward to 2014 and Brian telling me that one of the biggest sources of inspiration behind his own journey as an entrepreneur was the GSB (Graduate School of Business at Stanford) story about Marcos and MercadoLibre. He had read the case study and thought to himself: *Wow, this is similar to what I'm trying to do. I want to build the MercadoLibre of real estate.*

He said to me, "Linda, I want to help inspire others the way I was inspired. I want Endeavor to be a platform where I can give back and share more of my story."

That was music to my ears. I already knew that we wanted Viva Real to become part of our Endeavor network. People had been telling me that this guy, Brian, was really special—and he certainly was. As mentioned earlier, he had already made a big impact on the local tech market. But beyond that, he was someone who believed, like I did, in the power of success stories and the role-model effect. Just as Marcos had been influenced by Wences' underdog story with Patagon.com, Brian had been influenced by Marcos's internet success with MercadoLibre.

As Brian himself writes in the introduction to this book, "the spirit of entrepreneurship is to share with others." I couldn't agree more.

WHO AM I?

In the mid-nineties, I was in Brazil giving a talk and after speaking at length about Apple—about Steve Jobs and Steve Wozniak—people came up to me and said, essentially, "Nice story, Linda, but this thing about building a startup out of your garage, the whole Silicon Valley trope, doesn't resonate here. In Latin America, we don't even have garages." I realized then just how badly the region needed local role models. The reason people weren't becoming entrepreneurs was that it simply wasn't part of their daily reality, their shared experience.

Soon, I would learn it wasn't even part of their vocabulary.

After struggling to figure out the word in Spanish or Portuguese for "entrepreneur," I discovered that there wasn't one! At least not in the popular lexicon. The only term that people used regularly was *empresario*, which connoted an old-fashioned businessman.

Well, I thought, *this is the problem.* How could young people explain to their parents that they were going to be an entrepreneur if there wasn't even a word for it? I vowed to change that.

A number of years later, the editor of the Portuguese Brazilian Dictionary *Aurélio* called up our managing director at the time, Paulo Veras (who later became the founder of 99). Paulo happened to be in Brazil at the moment he got the call. The editor told him that, partly because of Endeavor's work with entrepreneurs, they were going to add the word *empreendedorismo* to their dictionary. How cool is that? From that point on, I became obsessed with the idea that we need words. It wasn't only Portuguese and Spanish. There was no word for "entrepreneurship" in lots of languages: Arabic, Turkish, Bahasa Indonesian. It seems crazy, right? Obviously, there are entrepreneurs all around the world. But back then, it was far from obvious.

In fact, when my co-founder, Peter Kellner, and I first started Endeavor, everyone thought it was a terrible idea. "There aren't any entrepreneurs in emerging markets," they would say. And if there were, they would never grow because there was no venture capital in emerging markets. So what was the point? That was the conventional wisdom back then.

It took some time, but eventually, we convinced the naysayers. And the way we did it was through *stories*—something that Brian understood instinctively.

BRIAN AND VIVA REAL

Obviously, it's weird to call Brazil—the fifth largest nation in the world—a "small pond." But in the tech world, it really was, and Brian was a big fish in this small pond. So when he came to Spain to one of our international selection panels that I was moderating, he was understandably pretty optimistic about his chances. I was too. But then the night before, I read the panelist scores, and an alarm went off: *Houston, we have a problem.* There was at least one panelist who was not convinced Viva Real was as great as everyone said. Not only that, but this person thought the company had been overvalued by the bubble of the Brazilian market at the time.

Look, it's true of every company that when you peel back the onion, there are going to be some question marks. I could tell that this fellow wanted to poke Brian a bit: he saw that Brian was a smart guy who had been told the valuation of his company was such-and-such. He wasn't trying to be mean, but he believed that Brian could use some tough love.

At Endeavor, we always have to have unanimous approval, but I had come to Spain confident that we would. In fact, I was expecting Brian's selection to take not much more than five minutes. Instead, it took two hours and was really contentious. One of the final casting votes came from the skeptical panelist. He said something to the effect of: "I just don't trust the technology, and we don't have the CTO here, so we have no way of knowing."

It was then that one of the other panelists and Endeavor entrepreneurs, Martin Migoya, CEO of Globant, came to Brian's rescue. He said, "Well, actually, I know their technology guy because he was a former Glober. And while I should be upset, the truth is I'm proud—and I can vouch for the technology. Which is why we must select Brian." Martin's words persuaded the other panelist, and Brian was indeed selected.

I was very happy with the resolution, not just because of the outcome but also the way it played out. First of all, it wasn't Brian's fault if Viva Real had been overvalued by a bubble in Brazil. Should a company be held responsible when a market is frothy? I don't think so. This is a question that came up a lot in the late 2010s. But back then—this was before SoftBank came on the scene—it was unchartered territory, and Brian just happened to be caught in the middle.

Was he overconfident? Perhaps. But how then do you tell someone that their selection is not the shoo-in they may have anticipated? You do it by giving them the good news and the bad news. In Brian's case, the good news was that he was now going to become an Endeavor entrepreneur. The bad news was that it was a really close call—but also an opportunity to think about what he could have done differently.

What I love about that story most of all, and what I will always remember, is how well it reflected on our ecosystem. Here was this small market where people were aggressively vying for talent. How remarkable, then, that the person who ended up vouching for Brian was the very guy who had recently lost one of his top technology people to Viva Real? Instead of feeling resentful at what could have been perceived as poaching, Martin was highly supportive. It made me feel proud and like we were all in this together, seeding this fertile ecosystem.

As for Brian, I knew all along that he was very deserving. And he knew that I had allowed the conversation to go on for longer than normal so as to get him selected. Later, when I met with him in my office in New York, we bonded even more. I learned, for example, about his unusual upbringing as the son of two parents with backgrounds in psychology. Apparently, after getting back from Spain, he had talked to his mom and dad to better understand why he might have come off as arrogant that day—it was so at odds with his own self-perception.

I was struck and impressed by Brian's openness and just how willing he was to analyze and critique himself to such a degree. The grueling selection process had made him question everything. But that's what being an entrepreneur is all about, and it's why Brian's book is so important and necessary. The story of almost every founder, especially with venture-backed companies, is one of ups and downs, ebbs and flows, and likely lots of mistakes. Then, of course, there are all the personal challenges, tough decisions, and enormous sacrifices to one's relationships, health, and much more.

You have come to this book because you want to hear the real deal. You crave those authentic voices and stories. And that's exactly what distinguishes Brian. Not only is he a terrific entrepreneur who has already made a big impact on Latin America's tech ecosystem. That alone is very important, of course. But what makes him really special is the honesty of his voice. He is willing to go where most of us won't to dig deeply and reckon with sometimes uncomfortable truths. We can all learn a great deal from the story of Viva Real and from the raw insights that Brian shares in the following chapters.

Simply put, you need to read this book. **Every entrepreneur needs to read this book.**

WHAT YOU WILL GET OUT OF IT

For readers who are familiar with Ben Horowitz's bestselling titles, think of *Viva the Entrepreneur* as *The Hard Thing About Hard Things* for Latin America.

In particular, Brian has learned a lot in the process of raising capital that he is now sharing with others as a way of balancing what he sees, rightly, as an information asymmetry. Venture capitalists do this every day of their lives, whereas entrepreneurs do it four or five times total. By definition, entrepreneurs have less experience. They need all the information they can get. In today's world, I believe it is more important than ever for entrepreneurs to ask questions up front about whether their potential funders want growth, or profitability, or both, and how fast, how far, and so on.

Brian shows entrepreneurs how to *push*—not only on the terms in the term sheet and the financial aspects but all the substantive decisions.

You need to know what's going to happen when the going gets tough. Do you trust your investors to look out for the long-term? Entrepreneurs have a ten- or twenty-year view of their business, but financial providers often have a much shorter time horizon. When everything's going well, everyone's in sync. The problem of misalignment only comes into focus during the tough times. And as I write this foreword for Brian in the midst of a global health and economic crisis, it certainly appears that tough times are on the horizon.

That is why Brian's advice here is so important. He teaches readers not only how to get the best valuation or the most money, but also how to ask the tough questions.

A NEW GENERATION OF *EMPREENDEDORES*

When Endeavor Brazil opened its first office in 2000, again, there was no popular word for "entrepreneur" and very few self-made examples in tech. To be clear, there *were* entrepreneurs in Brazil, and there have *always been* entrepreneurs in Brazil. But not really in tech. So when you look at someone like Brian or Paulo Veras of 99, their success is all the more impressive given how hard it was to raise capital back then. For funds like Redpoint and Monashees that got in early, it was hard too—because the Brazilian economy kept fluctuating.

Today, Brazil is taking its rightful seat on the global stage in terms of technology. Ten years ago, a Brazilian tech company would focus only on Brazil. Now, however, we're seeing Brazilian tech go global. And this is just the beginning. We're only scratching the surface with all the tech talent coming out of Brazil and all the strong, interesting, innovative companies in this sector.

The big question is, how do all these talented entrepreneurs—the ones already there as well as those to come—build companies in a *sustainable* way? This is where Brian's book can help founders think through the type of capital they want to raise, the type of investor they want to be in partnership with, and the mistakes they can hopefully avoid by learning from Brian's example.

It's great that Brazilian tech founders are finally going global. But it also means that they—you—need to be savvier and more introspective and willing to reflect on and learn from the mistakes of others. Thankfully, Brian has *been there*, through it all, and is now sharing his roller-coaster entrepreneur story, revealing his ups and downs, in the hopes of helping and inspiring us all.

As entrepreneurs, we're often taught to be extroverts. It makes some sense: we have to be selling all the time, selling our visions, our products, and services, selling people on why they should come work with us or why they should fund us. It is an outward-looking job where you're running a million miles an hour. How many of us have the time, skills, or fortitude to look more deeply inside ourselves?

What are our real motivations? How do we think about this thing that we're so passionately going after, day in and day out? And will our perception of ourselves change if, say, we take this round, expand too fast, fire this person, etc.? These are hard questions, but thankfully Brian has the inclination and tools to help us through them.

As tremendous an entrepreneur as he is, at heart, Brian is an educator who believes in the role-model effect and paying it forward. That is precisely what he has done with this essential book.

INTRODUCTION

Journey of a "Fundador"

It was a Tuesday morning—May 7, 2019—that I woke up and saw the email. "LOI" was the subject line: Letter of Intent. I took a deep breath and clicked on the attachment. It was what we call a *term sheet*, laying out the basics of the deal.

A $600–$700 million all-cash offer to negotiate the sale of our company, Grupo ZAP Viva Real.

Flash back one year: we had spent the entire first half of 2018 trying to raise money—and had *completely failed*. We had landed meetings with two highly respected investors, Warburg Pincus and General Atlantic, but didn't get far with either. In both cases, there was a significant gap in valuation from what we were expecting.

Looking back on it now, I probably should have taken the term sheet from General Atlantic and their legendary investor,

Martin Escobari. It wasn't anything close to $600+ million. In fact, it valued our company at a significant "down round," i.e., significantly lower than during our previous round of investment several years earlier. But if we had taken that capital from GA, maybe we could have reignited growth earlier—which would have given us more options and allowed us to sell the business at a much higher price in the future or keep operating and do an IPO in the US. There's no way to know, and in the end, what's done is done. That's the name of the game in entrepreneurship. You can't live with regrets; you just have to keep going.

During the process of fundraising post-merger, my sense was that the company was worth at least twice as much as what was being offered. But the feedback we received at the time was that our expectations—specifically mine and those of my successor as CEO, Lucas Vargas—were too high. That's just how the cookie crumbles when you go to market: like it or not, you find out where *the market thinks you are* in terms of value.

It was a rude awakening. The whole ordeal had been rather demoralizing. I felt like some of the members of our board were losing confidence in us.

But now, a year later, in May 2019, we were receiving an offer valued at *twice* the amount as before. It was a good offer, a fair offer. But to be frank, even the $600–$700 million felt low. Once again, it didn't meet my expectations, as well as the expectations of many of our existing investors. I knew that several of these individuals would make zero profit on the transaction: they were poised to just break even, meaning get their money back but nothing more.

All things considered, it may not have been the dream transaction I had been hoping for, but it *was* a 2X increase in value compared to when we had gone out to raise capital in early 2018. For that, I was grateful.

Still, I had mixed feelings: while a part of me was genuinely elated to see the market valuing us closer to what I believed to be fair, there was also something bittersweet about the thought of selling the company. It was like seeing your kids go off to college. When it came to the actual work we did at Grupo ZAP Viva Real, I felt like we still had so much unfinished business toward making a positive impact and transforming the real estate market.

As I contemplated all of this the morning I got the new offer, I looked at my laptop screen again and was jolted back to an even earlier memory.

In 2009, when we first started our business and launched the website, we were pursuing seed financing and had landed a meeting with the prominent tech investment firm, Tiger Global Management.

They flew out to Colombia, where we were located, and not five minutes into our meeting—we hadn't even had a chance to begin our presentation!—told us flat-out they were investing in our competitor, to the tune of $10 million. They encouraged us to refocus our business toward a different market geographically so as not to compete with their new investment.

To be clear, I hold nothing against Tiger for any of this. In fact, I appreciated their candor. They could have easily not disclosed this investment to us because it wasn't public and instead use the opportunity to gain sensitive information about our business for their own advantage. The fact that they didn't do that, and were open and transparent with us, is a testament to their professionalism as a firm.

To this day, I respect how Tiger handled that situation. But it certainly wasn't the result I had hoped for—and that's putting it mildly. To be honest, I was crushed. I went home that day and cried. I had put all my eggs in this basket. My wife and I had just sold our apartment and put the money from the sale into the business. It was almost everything we had. Now, I had to go home and break the news to her. Not only that, but my dear friend had also just put in a bunch of money, and so had my dad.

To add insult to injury, Tiger made us an informal offer to buy us out for about double what we had put in, which was about half a million dollars. It was a slap in the face, a way to stomp us out. In effect, they were sending us a message: we're going to crush you, and you should be grateful just to get your money back (with a small profit).

We didn't accept that offer.

Over the following years, we scaled our business and found great success, ultimately eclipsing that early competitor that Tiger had invested in.

But by early 2018, when we went out to the market and tried to raise money, we were experiencing new challenges. We had just merged Viva Real with ZAP, another huge real estate site in Brazil, and had suffered through the pains of that transition. The industrial logic for the deal was obvious, but anytime you put together two competitors of equal size who have been fighting it out for years, there are big challenges. Both companies had an inflated headcount and a lot of redundancy, and we ended up having to let go of 400 people. The result was that for the first time in many years, the forecast for our business was lukewarm. We were looking at flat or potentially negative growth. This is typically death to a venture-backed company.

In retrospect, trying to raise money at that juncture was problematic. Given that our business was in a temporary slump, some of the members on our board were willing to raise money at a significant discount. Meanwhile, many of us, myself included, had big expectations and were probably overly aggressive in terms of what we wanted to raise.

We just completely fell on our faces.

Which is why I think, in retrospect, I felt a sense of relief upon receiving the email the following May. It was as if hope had been restored. Through 2018, there had been a kind of gloom around our business, like the ship was sinking. For one thing, money had been pouring into some of our competitors: other real estate startups who were now perceived, right or wrong, as sexier than us. It didn't help matters either that our VP of engineering had almost been lured to another company. His role had been especially critical in a time when we were busy trying to integrate two very different technology platforms.

I recalled one month in particular, August 2018, when it felt like everything we had built, all that I had dreamed of, might come crashing down. Thinking back to that terrible time helped me put the new development in perspective: only nine months earlier, our business was filled with such uncertainty that its very existence seemed at risk, and now, here we were, in a much better situation.

Moreover, here we were *ten years* after initially launching our business and rejecting the informal bid that had been intended, indirectly, to kneecap us and take us out of the competition—with someone now offering six to seven hundred times that amount to buy our company!

Startups are the wildest roller coasters.

It's a weird feeling. **As an entrepreneur, you spend so much of your time carrying around the huge burden of all the people who made a bet on you, who believed and invested in you in the early days.** Then, in a single moment—*ta-dah!*—it all changes, and you realize you're going to potentially be making some of those people a *bunch of money.*

That alone was gratifying, even though my impulse in starting the business wasn't to get rich or make other people rich. Yes, the thought of having financial freedom is something I had always aspired to, but it wasn't why I became an entrepreneur.

BECOMING AN ENTREPRENEUR

I learned the word "entrepreneur" from my dad back when I was just a freshman in high school. At the time, I had started my own little business: private swim lessons at the pool behind my parents' house in Sebastopol, California.

The new word struck a chord with me. I identified it with what I was doing and where I wanted to go in life. But when I made the mistake of showing off my fancy word around my friends, they made fun of me for it: "Ohhh, so you're an entrepreneur now?" I probably deserved the gentle teasing that I received.

But it didn't stop me from saying and thinking about it all the time. The word stuck with me.

Many years later, after living in South America and building businesses there, I was fascinated to discover that "entrepreneur" in Portuguese—*empreendedor*—has only really existed in the popular lexicon for the past twenty years. (Before that, the word was just *empresário*, which calls to mind a staid businessman in a suit.)

In fact, it was the entrepreneur organization Endeavor and its Co-Founder/CEO Linda Rottenberg (who wrote the foreword of my book!) who helped popularize the word *emprendedor/ empreendedor* in Brazil and the rest of Latin America in the late nineties.

> The word in Spanish and Portuguese for entrepreneur— emprendedor/empreendedor—didn't exist in the popular lexicon until twenty years ago!

When I first traveled to Rio de Janeiro in 2001, I tried to speak Spanish (like most Gringos). People were polite, but I quickly realized Brazil is different. Despite being part of Latin America, I could see that the country had its own strong, unique identity. I loved the vibe of the people. During my short trip, I realized that I would go back to Brazil. I didn't know how or why, but a seed was planted, and I knew I was destined to return.

A few years later, at the age of twenty-three, I got in my car with a close friend and drove from California through Mexico and eventually to Costa Rica. From there, I sold my car and bought a one-way ticket to Colombia. My goal was to make it all the way down to Patagonia. But I also wanted to visit Andrea, who would later become my wife. I met her in college in San Diego. She was Colombian and, after graduating, had gone back to her home country.

My plan was to spend a few months in Colombia and make my way toward Brazil. But three months turned into seven years: Andrea and I got married and lived in Bogota until 2010. After a brief return to the States, we then moved to Brazil, where we soon started a family.

It was at this time that my love and passion for this region of the world came together in a big way with my lifelong desire to build my own company. I had started Viva Real, an online portal for real estate, a few years earlier and ran the business along with my co-founder Thomas Floracks out of Colombia, where the cost of living was low. But at a certain point, we made the decision to change up our focus from trying to serve many markets across Latin America to targeting the biggest one only: Brazil. Diego Simon founded the Brazil operation and led the business there until I was able to move there full-time.

Having wanted to be an entrepreneur ever since I learned the term from my dad, I had always been inspired to do my own thing, build value for myself, and chase my dreams. As mentioned earlier, I didn't start my business to get rich: my main motivation was to create something I could be proud of and make an impact.

This is important, and it's a lesson I'll explore further in the following chapters: if you start a business only driven by money, you'll be more likely to quit when things get tough.

> Money is indeed part of being an entrepreneur, but ideally, it's a by-product of being *passionate* about what you're doing.

For me, starting Viva Real, moving to Colombia, and later moving to Brazil was all an expression of this underlying passion. But even that passion was not always enough to fuel me through the tough times. My journey during these years, frankly, was filled with ups and downs. I often felt lost in the wilderness. It's different now: there is a great deal of information out there about how to build businesses. Ten years ago, however, these resources were few and far between. I sought guidance wherever I could get it.

To me, the spirit of entrepreneurship is to *share your experiences*, and I know that I have learned so much from others who have talked publicly and written about their successes and failures.

I believe this spirit of sharing and paying it forward is key to fostering healthy ecosystems. It's how the most solid entrepreneurial environments are nurtured: through the virtuous cycle of having success and then helping and reinvesting in future leaders.

In Latin America, this dynamic is still nascent. Yes, there have been many incredible people who came before me and shared their experiences and insights. **The social and economic landscape for incubating local entrepreneurship and helping it flourish remains in its early stages of development.**

I am compelled to see the region strive and thrive. Having given so much *to me*, I feel extreme gratitude to the region of Latin America and its people. In fact, out of the nearly forty investments I have made (at the time of this writing) as an angel investor, over 90 percent are in the region.

Not only am I betting on the current crop of entrepreneurs, I'm betting on the future of Latin America. I am convinced that with the talent and opportunities there, the future is bright for the entire region. I believe entrepreneurship is a huge lever for social mobility and prosperity, and I am fully committed to helping bring about these changes.

> The spirit of thriving startup ecosystems is for founders to share their experiences, pay it forward, and reinvest in future leaders.

Over the past decade, I have been afforded the luxury of supporting myself and my family through work and opportunity born in this region—and again, for that, I am extremely grateful. It is a market that historically has been neglected as a center of focus for investors and entrepreneurs. This is not for lack of talent. Latin America just hasn't been on the radar for a lot of people, and again, its entrepreneurial ecosystem is still in its infancy. But this is changing, and it is changing fast!

Although the economic fallout from the coronavirus pandemic of 2020 will almost certainly pose big challenges in the region for entrepreneurs and investors, we will also likely see new opportunities born out of the crisis. I'm reminded of how, in Northern California where I live, we have been hit with lots of wildfires in recent years. These annual occurrences have been devastating to our community in many ways, but one remarkable phenomenon is that there is a specific flower here which appears only after a fire: the gorgeous and rare hollyhock "Baker's globe mallow," known for how it blooms out of burnt earth.

I see this as a nice symbol for how something beautiful can flourish out of the ashes of chaos and disaster, and the reality is that—no matter what challenges lie ahead—I remain optimistic about Latin America's ecosystem, bullish that over the coming years and decades, many jobs will be created, the middle class will grow, and prosperity will expand through the region. This is not a statement on the region's politics (as that is a complicated topic not for this book) but rather is rooted in my firm belief that entrepreneurship can have a meaningful impact on society.

I want to be a part of *all* of this. What about you?

FINDING YOUR WAY

You have come to this book, of course, because you have an interest in building a business in Latin America. Maybe you're a founder or an aspiring founder, an early employee at a tech company. You feel a bit lost, like I did. Insecure. Unsure of what it takes or what your priorities need to be as you move forward along this path. The journey can be lonely.

Maybe at this stage, you just have an *idea* for a business. Or maybe you already have your engineers and are building your MVP (Minimum Viable Product). **Wherever you may be on your own journey—of founding, scaling, and raising venture capital in Latin America—it is my humble hope that you can use this book as the resource I wish someone had given me.**

It is worth pointing out here that raising venture capital, in particular, is not for everyone. There are certain types of businesses and startups that definitely *shouldn't* be raising capital from outside investors, and I will explain these distinctions in depth in the following chapters.

Whether or not *you* are raising capital, the insights in Part Three and throughout the book will, I believe, be interesting and informative for readers and entrepreneurs of all stripes.

Another important caveat: what I put forth in these pages is certainly not the *only* way to pursue your journey. Nor is the book intended as a strict instructional manual. But it does have plenty of specific, actionable advice and takeaways about how to structure your business, how to frame the crucial decisions you're going to have to make, how to hire good people, and even items like how to create a stock option plan.

Ultimately, what I hope you take from the following chapters is a healthy dose of inspiration—so that you don't feel alone in the struggle—as well as some nuggets of insight to help you prepare for future situations and challenges (or even to give you a new perspective on something that has already happened).

Throughout the book, I draw from my own entrepreneurial story to show how my trials and tribulations growing my business, Viva Real, will likely resonate with *your* day-to-day experiences—whether you're still in the planning stage or in the middle of your business's life cycle or have already been through it.

Again, I've made *many* mistakes along my journey, as will soon be revealed. I am not writing as someone who holds all the answers or has done everything right. The book is meant not as business gospel but rather as loose principles based on all I've learned from my successes and failures—as well as the valuable lessons I've absorbed from my own mentors.

When I was starting out, **I had no idea what the different terms**

in a term sheet meant. I had to go to Wikipedia to get the definitions! Eventually, however, I was able to build relationships with some amazing teachers who showed me the way. It took a long time, but once I had access to these people and their hard-earned expertise, it made all the difference.

When I think back to ten or fifteen years ago, the truth is I would have never imagined how much I would learn through the whole process.

You can, too. Part of it is throwing yourself into the deep end and figuring out how to swim by just doing it. But part of it is also learning from others. I am very fortunate to have had people (including many investors in my company) who were very generous with their time and advice.

Now, with this book, I want to do for you what they did for me.

THE REAL DEAL

Let me be clear: even with all the resources in the world, your journey is not going to be a walk in the park. I don't want to sugarcoat it. Founding and scaling a business, raising capital… these are hard things. The life of an entrepreneur is stressful. There are a lot of unknowns. It can be highly demoralizing.

For me, however, and hopefully for you too, what makes it all worth it is the creative process, the opportunity to challenge yourself and overcome obstacles. **Building your own business is the ultimate accelerator for personal and professional growth.**

I know that I've constantly been surprised by what the people I've worked with and I have been able to accomplish together, how *much* we are capable of. Brazil's most successful entrepreneur and investor, Jorge Paulo Lemann, has a saying, "It costs the same amount of energy to dream small and dream big. So, dream big!" It all starts with having a belief in something. Dreaming big allows you to achieve big. If you dream small, you will achieve small.

⸘ Look for where the BIG potential lies. ⸘

Latin America, of course, is a part of the world with incredible potential. But the longer you wait, sitting on the sidelines, the more likely someone else is going to come in and leverage those opportunities.

Take action now. Why *shouldn't* it be you who achieves big?

I get it; maybe you're not sure you have what it takes. Maybe you didn't go to the best school or get the best grades. Well, guess what? Neither did I!

It may have become a cliché, but I wholeheartedly agree with what the great American entrepreneur Thomas Edison said about genius: it's 1 percent inspiration and 99 percent perspiration. I have seen some of the smartest people lose out on opportunities. They had all the potential in the world but didn't seize it.

As for me, when I first moved to Latin America, I didn't know anyone. I hardly had any money. But I grinded and hustled. I worked *hard* and stayed at it. I didn't do it alone, but it did feel lonely.

You are going to have your own ups and downs, no doubt about it. But as long as you're clear-eyed about the challenges and willing to endure the pain—and embrace the spirit of *going after it* and *doing the damn thing* with grit and tenacity—you are as capable as anyone of making an enormous impact.

Believe in yourself. As an entrepreneur, you need to have a level of determination and conviction that, at times, borders on egotistical. But you also need to listen, *really* listen. Have the humility to learn from others and the courage to ask for advice.

If I could do it all, so can you.

I will show you how.

MANAGING YOUR PSYCHOLOGY

CHAPTER ONE

THE BEST DAY OF YOUR LIFE AND THE WORST IN *THE SAME DAY*

Building a business is an emotional roller coaster like no other, and the life of a founder, particularly with venture-backed companies, is often filled with stress, anxiety, loneliness, and isolation—it's not for everyone! It requires a certain obsessiveness, a degree of "crazy" that is in the DNA of many entrepreneurs and can be its own superpower. If you're driven primarily by money, you'll be more likely to quit when the going gets tough. You have to be passionately motivated by the greater purpose behind what you're doing—and you have to lean on a support network of other entrepreneurs and mentors like Brian does with his "Breakfast Club." You must also be willing to open up and show vulnerability, especially with your angel investors. Brian leaned heavily on advisors like Simon Baker, who had already done what he was trying to do (in a different region, Australia) and could provide a helpful roadmap. He also learned through his own mistakes the value of transparency and why you shouldn't shield your team or co-founders from challenges and problems in your business.

In 2014, I wrote a personal letter to Ben Horowitz, the famed entrepreneur and co-founder of the venture capital firm Andreessen Horowitz. I had just read his book, *The Hard Thing About Hard Things*, which struck a deep nerve in me—especially the parts about the stress and anxiety, loneliness and isolation, that he and other CEOs so often feel.

I had been going through my own challenges at the time, which I described to him in my letter. Ironically, **I had recently been named Entrepreneur of the Year in Brazil**, and Viva Real had just raised a bunch of money—but I felt like we were wasting a lot of it.

It was a weird patch in my life and for our company. From the outside, everything looked rosy. I was seen as a success story for having won the award, and it solidified Viva Real's status at the highest level of the Brazilian startup ecosystem. But the contrast with my mood internally couldn't have been starker. We were still in a piece of shit building. There had just been a power outage where we lost electricity for days on end. *Everything* was falling apart in the office, from the building itself to how we were (or rather weren't) communicating with our customers.

I remember feeling really down in the dumps and upset by the gap between perception and the reality behind the scenes. For a few days, I could hardly even get out of bed. Then, the night of the awards ceremony, I was supposed to make a little speech but could barely string together a handful of words. As soon as it was over, I ducked out of the venue. My mind was too wrapped up in all the business challenges to even appreciate the moment.

On paper, it should have been the *best day ever* for Viva Real and me. We were being honored by our esteemed community of founders and investors and singled out from among all Brazilian startups for special recognition.

But strangely, it felt more like *the worst day ever.*

I guess it was both. That's just how it is for entrepreneurs. On the one hand, it's what makes it so exciting: the best day of your life and the worst all in the same day. **But it's enough to give you whiplash!** I've heard the same sentiment from many entrepreneurs. Maybe they wake up in the morning and get some terrible news, but then in the afternoon, receive their biggest contract ever.

Building a business is an emotional roller coaster like none other.

THIS LIFE IS NOT FOR EVERYONE

Lots of first-time entrepreneurs fall in love with the *idea* of being their own boss. They're motivated by the romantic dream of it, the supposed flexibility, and not having to answer to anyone. But the reality is very different. If you're not careful, you can end up a slave to your own projects. In fact, your stress and anxiety can be much higher than if you worked for someone else.

There's nothing wrong with starting a company because you want to be your own boss but understand that what you're really after is a *lifestyle business*—something that generates a good bit of cash and can finance your lifestyle. It's a perfectly valid path for some people. But it's not what this book is about.

In the following chapters, you're going to read about what it takes to start and scale a different kind of business, the kind where there is **an enormous growth opportunity that will attract people who want to be involved in it, whether investors or top talent looking to build something ambitious and transformative.**

With businesses like these—in contrast to lifestyle businesses—stress and anxiety are par for the course. This is especially true with venture-backed companies, where you must always have accountability to your investors. Don't get me wrong; you can still be in control of your own destiny. But I'm not going to lie; it's a difficult life. If your primary motivation for such an undertaking is to make money, well this is probably not the best way to do that. Let me be clear: I am a capitalist, and there isn't anything wrong with wanting to make a bunch of money. The problem, as mentioned in the introduction, is that when you're driven by money above all else, it makes it that much harder to get through those difficult moments you'll inevitably face.

You need to have a greater purpose for *why* you're doing what you're doing.

I suspect many of you already *do* have this understanding. You're motivated to build something intrinsically larger, at scale, that can have an exponential impact. But that also means you're probably going to need some capital—and once you raise capital, it changes the dynamics. It becomes that much harder to find a healthy balance.

As an entrepreneur, when you're going after something so ambitious, the truth of the matter is you're going to need to work your butt off constantly just to have *any* chance of overcoming all the obstacles ahead. Even then, there are no guarantees. Being willing to do whatever it takes, whenever it's needed, is not optional. It's the baseline. You certainly can't just shut off when the day is over, like in a regular job where you're working for someone else.

> Are you looking to build something transformative, or do you really just want to have a lifestyle business?

To be clear: balance *is* important, and ideally, you will find what works for you. We'll talk more about that in chapter two. But if balance is what you're looking for from the get-go as your main objective, I'm sorry to say that you're probably destined to fail.

I certainly don't encourage or condone working yourself to death. But know what you're getting into: **the life of a venture-backed entrepreneur is heavily tilted toward working around the clock, hustling on weekends, and waking up in the middle of the night because your mind is racing trying to solve a particular business problem.**

You can be sure that if you are a founder of a venture-backed business where you're raising capital and going after a tremendously large opportunity, you are going to have *many* of those sleepless nights. If you have a family to support, the stress is probably going to be even worse. Knowing that they depend on you to pay the bills and maybe don't believe in the business as much as you do, makes the pressure even more intense. For this reason, it is essential that you, as the founder, get buy-in from your family. You must always be candid with your loved ones about how much your endeavor is going to impact them. If not, it will come back to bite you.

Thankfully, there are tools you can use and skills you can develop to negotiate these challenges within yourself and not let the stress and anxiety overcome your whole life, like it almost did with me on numerous occasions.

Most important of all: don't keep the pressure bottled up. Share your challenges with others.

BUILDING A COMMUNITY

One of the most important actions you can take in warding off the stress-filled isolation that plagues so many entrepreneurs is to find your personal support network, made up of trusted individuals who you can really talk to. I recommend seeking other founders who have done what you are doing, have been through similar situations, and can offer their guidance in a non-judgmental way.

No man is an island, as they say, and I've leaned heavily on others throughout my life and career. In fact, one of the first people who played this role for me was someone I knew when I was still at university. As students at San Diego State, my close friend, James, and I started a carpet company together. At the time, we lived in the dorms. These residences were nothing to write home about. Worse were the crappy linoleum floors. One day, I had the idea of going to Sid's Carpet Barn and picking up a bunch of cheap remnant carpets. James was my roommate, and I recruited him to come with and convince the Carpet Barn to give us all these remnants on consignment.

The plan worked: after obtaining the carpets, we would sit out in front of the dorm on the first day of school and sell them to parents dropping off their kids. Over the following weeks, more and more students would come and buy them from us. We did this at the beginning of every semester, and our scheme became hugely successful.

Flash forward to senior year. Now, James and I were living together in the same house. We were always dreaming up business ideas together. We had another roommate, a Dutch guy who was working at an internet startup. James and Paul had the idea to build an online ticketing business. They invited me to join them, but I followed my heart instead.

Long story short: my two roommates went to London in 2003 to launch the ticket business. I didn't join them. Instead, I decided to opt-out of the project and drove with another close friend to Mexico, then to Costa Rica on a six-month adventure. Eventually, as you know from the introduction, I flew to Colombia to visit Andrea, who would later become my wife.

This turn of events with my friends and me was pivotal: not only because of how the decision set in motion my own entrepreneurial journey in South America but also because of what happened with the ticketing business. After moving to London, my two former roommates recruited another friend, who basically took my spot in the trio. The business did incredibly well, and a few years later, they sold it to Ticketmaster and made a ton of money.

My longtime friend James became a multimillionaire at age twenty-seven and invested some of his money in my new company. But it was more than that. He was the first person I really leaned on, not just financially but for his wisdom. He had already been through a lot of the process of building a business, fundraising, and more. (As an investor, his experience also lent some credibility to my project, even though he was still very young.)

At a time early in my career, when I was struggling to get off the ground, James was a great person to talk to about challenges and just general strategy, having built an online business himself.

I also leaned on my dad a lot in those early years. He is an entrepreneur, and much of my inspiration comes from him. At the time, he had a small paving company in my hometown. In high school, I used to work for him during the summer, doing hard labor. (My dad was also an early source of capital for Viva Real, along with James.)

Both of these individuals—James and my dad—were hugely helpful to me when I was starting out. They gave me my first guidance as an entrepreneur. Soon, however, my support group would grow to include the investors Simon Baker and Greg Waldorf, who I will talk about in more detail in the following chapters. The advice I received from these two was a bit more professionalized, in that they were both savvy investors with deep experience in almost exactly what I was trying to do. Their help was critical early on. Not only did they give money and credibility—social proof—but a real roadmap for me on how to build a business.

Later in my career, **I would lean on many others, mentors as well as peers in various entrepreneur organizations as an antidote to the persistent feelings of stress and isolation.**

There's no sugarcoating it: "lonely-at-the-top" may be a cliché, but it's 100 percent true. To survive the anxiety-filled life of an entrepreneur, especially if you're a founder of a venture-backed business, you have to develop coping mechanisms for protecting yourself from collapse. You can't do it on your own. You need friends, mentors, support groups.

Who in your business circle has done what you are trying to do and come out on the other side? And how do you even approach someone like that? It's one thing if you already have a Simon Baker type in your circle, but if not, how do you go about seeking them out? Many founders make the mistake of not reaching out to people they don't know, assuming these successful individuals would be too busy or wouldn't care about their project. This is sometimes true, but more often than not, you'd be surprised at just how open and receptive folks like this are.

That said, there is a skill to reaching out and developing the kind of relationships that ultimately lead to some form of mentorship. A good rule of thumb is: *if you want money, ask for advice; if you want advice, ask for money.* In my case, being able to tell my story well made all the difference in finding mentors and, eventually, capital. I told the story of what I wanted to build and where I wanted to go and found people who were in a position to help me—who were already connected to real estate and tech in some capacity.

The point is: *you* need to get *them* to take an interest in you, and that means figuring out what it is that will motivate them to help you.

But remember: getting these individuals to give you their time is just the beginning. In order to take away valuable lessons and insights from the relationships, you also have to be willing to open yourself up and show *vulnerability.*

THE POWER OF VULNERABILITY

Being vulnerable and letting others in on your anxieties and insecurities can be very difficult for a lot of people. Granted, it is not always appropriate to come across as a completely open book. It depends on your audience. Even among your investors, who I believe are a great source of support and guidance, you probably want to reveal different levels of vulnerability with an angel investor versus an institutional investor. The former is someone who is in your corner 100 percent. The latter is in your corner, too, but in a different way. Their relationship with you is somewhat more transactional.

Of course, you don't want *anyone* to think that you don't know what you're doing. Investors need to see that you have good ideas and clarity on what you're trying to build. But it's also important to show you're capable of listening and incorporating feedback. If an investor is going to get involved and try to help your business, they're going to want to know that you'll be receptive to what they have to say.

Especially when you're trying to get someone across the finish line to invest in your company, you need to express a level of humility. **There's a big difference between looking like you know what you're doing and acting like you *think* you know everything** (which is a big turnoff). That may seem obvious, but you'd be surprised how many people try to project an aura of all-knowingness as a kind of smokescreen, which comes across like they've really got something to hide.

For what it's worth, this behavior is common among investors too. I remember one time sitting with a bunch of venture capitalists from across Latin America, and the question came up: how open to coaching should founders be? The context was that a certain investor felt like one of the founders in the room wasn't listening to his feedback. Maybe so. But the reality, I've found, is that many investors *think* they know more about operating a startup than they actually do. They believe they're right, and the founder is wrong when the real problem is that, from their limited vantage point, they just don't have the full view on all the complicated decisions that have to be made in a startup.

Not all investors are like this, of course. For example, some have deep experience starting and scaling startups or significant operating experience in a specific sector. But even then, it's unrealistic in the short-term for them to try to dissuade a founder of his or her convictions. Good investors know this.

As for the investor in the room that day, he was well-intentioned but also, to my eyes, inexperienced.

Investors may sometimes be pushy, but that doesn't mean you shouldn't give serious consideration to their advice—even if you ultimately reject it. In my case, my investors saw that I was really listening, evaluating, and embracing their feedback and also implementing at least some of the changes they recommended. This made them feel more connected to my story and what I was doing—and inspired them to further help and support me.

But there were also times when I held firm in spite of opposition from investors. For example, I remember debating with Hernan Kazah from Kaszek Ventures (who is also the co-founder of MercadoLibre) our plan to limit the geographic focus of Viva Real and concentrate only on Brazil. Hernan had lived a different story at MercadoLibre and understandably had a different perspective. He questioned me pretty intensely about why it wouldn't be preferable to focus on several markets in parallel.

I remained adamant that we needed to go all-in on Brazil, and when he saw that I wasn't changing my mind—and also that I had good, solid reasoning behind my arguments—he quickly accepted my position.

In that scenario, I was right to trust in myself and what I strongly believed to be the best direction for our business. But there were plenty of other times when I didn't listen to Hernan and others, and I really should have! Sometimes founders just need to learn by *doing*, especially when it comes to letting themselves be vulnerable.

Over the following years, I came to learn the power of vulnerability, particularly when it came to my team. I learned that if you seek out smart people from a place of humility, acknowledging all that you don't know, you'll be amazed at how much they give and how willing they are to help you. The key is to just be really curious and always ask lots of questions.

When we were making our first executive hires, I ended up hiring three brilliant people who were all fresh out of Harvard Business School: Sasha, Lucas, and Renata. Clearly, these were exceptionally talented individuals. But the group dynamic wasn't great at first. The environment felt competitive. So, one day I showed the team a now-famous TED talk by Brené Brown called "The Power of Vulnerability." I thought it might help everyone let down their guards a bit.

The video didn't get the reaction I had hoped for. They may not have come right out and said it, but somehow I could tell that Sasha, Lucas, Renata, and others saw the TED talk as too fluffy, not mission-critical. Or at least that's what it seemed like at the time. It wasn't until a few years later that I spoke to Lucas again, and in greater detail, about the subject of vulnerability. By then, he had really started to absorb and appreciate this business principle of opening up and letting people in. Same with Sasha and Renata. In fact, all three evolved into incredible leaders—and just fantastic human beings who I have learned a lot from.

> Vulnerability isn't something they teach in business school, but it is such an important part of building trust and creating a strong team dynamic.

Learning to be vulnerable helped me in all of my relationships—including my team and various mentors. We've already talked about how much you can learn by opening yourself up to your investors, but often you can learn even *more* from other operators. For example, I had an investor named Shaun Di Gregorio, who was the CEO of a market-leading business in Malaysia that was equivalent to what we were trying to build in Brazil. In the early days of Viva Real, when I was thinking heavily about strategy, I flew out to Malaysia in a seventy-two-hour whirlwind trip, stayed at Shaun's house, and just hammered him with every question possible: how did he build his sales teams, what did his sales process look like, etc.? I took notes constantly.

When I came home, I referred back to these notes often. **Here was someone who had literally done what I was trying to do, and he basically handed me the roadmap.** How awesome is that?

Earlier, I had experienced something similar when Simon Baker flew down to Sao Paulo and shared *tons* of details about everything he had learned as the CEO of REA Group. Over the course of two full days, he sat with us and broke it all down, from industry marketing to consumer marketing, sales to product, and much more. After realizing just how much I had learned from Simon over those two days, I realized how valuable these meet-ups could be. That was when I decided to take the opportunity to fly to Malaysia and soak up everything I could from Shaun.

During this period, I also focused on getting institutional investors who had local experience, geographically speaking. As an American in Brazil, it made a big difference to have Brazilian or at least South American investors to help me navigate the market where I was now operating.

Would any of this have been possible if I hadn't shown vulnerability? To be fair, I probably *wasn't* very vulnerable or humble the first time I communicated with Shaun or Simon or Hernan or Greg. I'm sure the vibe I conveyed was more wild-eyed conviction and ambition than anything else. But I did always try to show them how much I valued their help in navigating the unfamiliar waters of building a startup in Latin America. Admittedly, the humility piece came more gradually, but in the end, it was equally important.

The way I look at it now, humility (or rather its opposite, pride) is like a glass of water. If your glass is already full to the top, you can't let in any new water. You have to pour a little out first to make room for the additional knowledge that you take from others.

Remember, no one expects you to know everything. Just being okay with that is in itself an advantage because it opens you up and allows for that inbound knowledge.

I try to practice this level of vulnerability each and every day.

But clearly, I wasn't always great at it. In fact, one of my biggest mistakes, I can see now, is that I became so focused on helping my team develop vulnerability and supporting *them* that I took my eye off the ball of this principle in myself.

TRANSPARENCY AND DELEGATION

As much as I've sought out trusted mentors and peers I can share with, a longstanding Achilles' heel of mine is that, internally, I tend to hold on to the challenges of building a business, making them all *my* problem.

It took me forever to figure this out but, eventually, I came to realize that **when you spread out these concerns among your team, people step up!** They may not have the same emotional investment that you do as a founder, but they want to know what's really going on with the business so they can help. When things are looking bad, you need to bring them in and not just keep it to yourself.

This became very clear to me at one point when I hid the truth from my co-founder, Thomas, about how bad things were really looking for our company in terms of cash flow. This was before we brought on our third partner, Diego. It was during the time we were making the transition from a website design and marketing services business to a real estate marketplace/classifieds business, Viva Real. Money was a stress and a challenge. Sometimes, we almost ran out of it completely. In theory, both Thomas and I were responsible for the money. But I was CEO, and the number one job of a CEO in early-stage companies is to make sure you have enough money.

At first, I *did* tell him what was going on. I distinctly remember sitting in his apartment, feeling really stressed-out, and saying to him, "Dude, we're kind of fucked. This might blow up."

With the cat now out of the bag, my preoccupation with our dwindling cash flow became his too, and he was *really* worried. The problem was I didn't actually want him to get freaked out. I feared it would affect his ability to perform. So from then on, I took a lot of the burden on myself. He already knew we were in trouble, so I couldn't hide it completely. But I didn't let on quite how bad it was. I kept the stress bottled up inside me and assured him we would work it out. My logic was that I didn't want to compound his stress—which would, in turn, compound the stress on me because now I'd be dealing with comforting him and myself!

I realize now how foolish my thinking was. I shouldn't have taken on all that burden. Thomas would have been fine! In fact, keeping it to myself was bad for our relationship as friends and co-founders. At one point, he told me I was internalizing too much.

He saw it, but I didn't.

In my mind, I was doing something admirable, trying to save someone else from the stress. But when you do that, not only do you isolate people, but you overload yourself. What I discovered later, to my surprise, was that people *can* take on a lot. They can help.

Don't shield other people from the challenges and problems in your business.

Now, of course, you don't want to be so open that you scare people away. Telling your co-founder is one thing; telling prospective employees is another. No one will come on board! You *do* have to filter to a certain degree. But on the whole, I definitely lean toward the principle of transparency.

What it comes down to is this: you have to know your audience.

I found *my* perfect audience when I linked up with four other entrepreneurs.

What really helped me learn how to be transparent and vulnerable was meeting up for breakfast once a month with David Vélez (Nubank), Thomaz Srougi (Dr. Consulta), Daniel Hatkoff (Pitzi), and Kimball Thomas (Dinda). We had the kind of shared experience that allowed us to bond amazingly fast. It's hard for others to understand what it takes to build a business. Just having an open forum to share what was on our minds was so great. The level of trust was just extraordinary. For example, when I decided to transition from CEO to chairman and spend more time in the US, I had a lot of worries about the decision. I felt like I was letting people down. This culminated in my having a small anxiety attack, which I shared with my Breakfast Club group.

One of the four entrepreneurs, Thomaz, who ran a network of health clinics, was especially supportive during that time. He thanked me for sharing what I was going through, and I remember feeling like I had truly been heard. It is hard when you feel alone in the struggle, and just being able to share this can help release some of the anxiety.

Of course, we also discussed more practical matters at our

Breakfast Club, like how we were dealing with our boards, or with investors, or with stock options—and those conversations were useful too. It helped enormously to hear how these other entrepreneurs had handled similar situations.

Even when what was being shared was not explicitly emotional or sensitive, there was just something about the dialogue in this Breakfast Club that made us feel supported. No one was throwing their egos around. We all were dealing with our own insecurities.

§ We *all* have insecurities.   §

Me, I admit I've always felt insecure about my academic background. Often, it seems like everyone you meet in the tech space either went to Stanford or Harvard. Seriously, there was a period of my life where every businessperson I encountered came from one of those business schools. Whereas I barely got through state college—a *very* state college—and took zero business classes.

I can't remember if I shared this particular insecurity with my Breakfast Club group, but I definitely had a valuable conversation about it with my investor, Greg Waldorf. He told me, "I'll take someone with your scrappy hustle mentality over any MBA." To hear that from him meant so much. It wasn't easy to expose myself in that way—especially to someone who himself had an MBA from Stanford—but if I hadn't done so, I would never have received those words of support.

Everyone is different, and it's easier for some people to show vulnerability than others. I was already pretty open to talking about my feelings because of my family background. My mom was a psychotherapist for years. She and my dad actually met in their early twenties when they were counselors together in a residential treatment center for emotionally disturbed children. Soon after they married, they began a master's program in psychology. Later, my mom became a bereavement counselor. Both my parents are just very equipped to dig into emotions.

Growing up in the Requarth household, my brother and I definitely absorbed these lessons and were probably more in touch with our feelings than the average kids. **I learned how effective and powerful it can be to share what's going on with you emotionally**—which makes it all the more ironic that I struggled later on, as I mentioned earlier, with practicing internally the same vulnerability that I was trying to bring out in my team.

It took time for me to get it right. But the truth is that even today, although I have a great support system and so many people I trust and can share with, there are still moments when I just feel terrible, like everything's going to come crashing down. I still question myself big time.

This chapter has been about managing stress and anxiety, and it's important to note that I say *managing*, not *overcoming*— because to a certain degree, stress and anxiety just come with the territory.

Again, this life is not for everyone. You have to be a little crazy to want to start and run your own company.

EMBRACING THE "CRAZY"

Linda Rottenberg says that in the startup world, "Crazy is kind of a compliment," and I agree. It's in our DNA. In fact, there have been studies by my friend Dr. Michael Freeman and others around the mental health differences that are a common part of the profile of entrepreneurs, and how they are significantly more likely to have ADHD, bipolar disorder, depression, and other mental health conditions—either themselves or in their families (i.e., a genetic predisposition). The data is quite compelling.

But what I find most interesting is how the positive traits associated with these conditions can become their own kind of superpower. For example, there's something called hypomania, which is a mood state characterized by persistent energy, creativity, motivation, and mood elevation. It's not full-on mania, but it's similar (though less intense). People with hypomania tend to experience bursts of euphoria as well as prolonged periods of staying focused on achieving their goals. It has been shown that a lot of entrepreneurs have this condition, and in many ways, it is a positive quality, but also clearly a double-edged sword.

Full disclosure: I am pretty sure I have a moderate case of hypomania. I definitely have moments when I get obsessed and go on a work bender. It's good and bad: **I am just so energized when I'm on to an idea, but admittedly I go a little crazy.**

I also relate to the hypomania trait of extreme optimism, over-confidence even, which can lead entrepreneurs to believe that really difficult tasks will not be as difficult as they seem. Maybe that's why you don't see many highly analytical types in entrepreneurial roles. Obviously, that's a generalization, and of course, you have to be somewhat analytical to even have the capability to start a business. Nonetheless, I have found—and this is just my anecdotal hypothesis—that there's a certain kind of individual, rigorously intellectual and logical to a fault, that you *don't* see much in the world of entrepreneurs because they are constantly anticipating everything that will go wrong.

For better or worse, people who think that way usually end up not taking action—and that can be an obstacle to success. It's ironic: even though they may be smarter in a sense, better able to assess risk, which is indeed important in entrepreneurship, they lack the bold conviction in themselves and their ideas.

People who have hypomania can almost block out the negative aspects of analytic risk assessment so that what could be described as a flaw or blindness to reality becomes, once again, a superpower.

Steve Jobs was famous for this. His admirers called it his "reality distortion field." Few have used it as successfully as Jobs, but I believe it's a quality that's more common among entrepreneurs than people may realize.

While this and other distinct characteristics of many entrepreneurs may indeed turn out to be secret weapons in their arsenal, the very same traits can make it hard to live a balanced, well-rounded life, as we'll see in the following chapter.

CHAPTER TWO

WHAT REALLY MATTERS

Brian's wife, Andrea, had always been "in it to win it" with him—but when he got swept up in building his business, it started to put some pressure on the marriage. He made a vow to himself to not blow it with the people who mattered most: his family (which now included a child). By this point, his work had gotten so out of control that he felt like a man possessed. He made a conscious decision to change his ways, such as committing to be home in time for dinner four nights a week. Brian encourages readers to temper their hypomanic entrepreneurial brain with a dose of cautious self-awareness so that your obsession doesn't consume you entirely. He shows how to deliberately shut off and let your brain rest, which can lead, ironically, to creative breakthroughs with your work. But this can only happen if you consciously establish routines and set strict boundaries around how you spend your days. These were lessons that Brian had to learn gradually over time and many ups and downs (including a debilitating panic attack), but now he sees clearly that when you're working nonstop on nights and weekends, you're actually not that productive!

The year was 2009. Along with my two co-founders, Thomas and Diego (who I brought on earlier that year), I was in the thick of trying to build our business. Andrea and I were still living in Colombia at the time, and Diego was the only person we had on the ground in Brazil, which had turned out to be, without a doubt, our most important market.

It was a stressful time. We didn't have any money, so whenever I'd come to Brazil, I'd just stay at Diego's apartment in Sao Paulo. The interpersonal dynamics of staying with someone when you're also in a work environment with that person can be tricky. It was mostly typical roommate stuff, but it felt even more chaotic because of the chaos we were experiencing trying to grow the business.

Then, in February of 2010, Andrea came with me on one of these trips, and we spent almost four weeks with Diego and his wife, sleeping in the living room of his small, one-bedroom apartment. Even with her there, I was working day and night.

In Sao Paulo, there are often torrential rainstorms in the summer months (Dec–Feb), and I will never forget one particular moment when Andrea and I were in the lobby of Diego's building about to head out. We stopped in our tracks: the rain outside was just crazy. Sheets of water *sweeping* across everything. It looked like a river in the street.

The sight of it triggered something in Andrea, and she started crying. "What the hell are we doing here?" she said. "This is ridiculous!"

You have to understand; my wife is pretty much a rock. She is amazingly tough and resilient. But it was as if the streams of rainwater outside the window had finally given her permission to release her own tears and say out loud what had been building up inside her.

It hit me right in my gut to see my wife like that. But I pulled it together and tried to comfort her: "You've got to trust me. This *is* going to work out."

That was a pivotal moment in our relationship, a real test. We had been married for about five years at that point and were both pretty young, relatively speaking, when we tied the knot. **It wasn't long after the wedding that I started to get really caught up in the business, and over the following years, she never questioned what I was trying to do.**

Until now.

It didn't make matters any less stressful that after recently deciding we wanted to have a baby together, we were having trouble getting pregnant. On top of that, we were trying to conceive *while staying at my co-founder's apartment*—where we didn't even have our own room and had to, um, get creative.

Meanwhile, Andrea had applied for American citizenship, and with that process, you are required to live in the country six months out of the year. At the time, our plan had been to move to the US, but then it turned out that my co-founders and I were starting the business in Brazil. So with Andrea in the States for half of the year, I had to go back and forth.

She had her mother with her in California, so she wasn't completely alone. (Andrea's mom had lived with us in one locale or another since 2006, and she still does. She is the best. I like to say that when I got married, I got a package deal—two for one!) But the distance between Andrea and me and the constant traveling added more stress to an already stressful situation, especially with me hard at work trying to raise money for the business in Brazil—and it definitely tested our marriage.

It wasn't until that day in 2010, however, with the storm raging outside, that these issues came to a head.

I will always remember the scene in the apartment lobby. After assuring her that everything would be okay, that we would get through it, I paused and let Andrea take a moment to gather her thoughts. Then, in an instant, she wiped away her tears, looked up at me, and nodded. She didn't have to say anything. I knew her well enough to understand the meaning behind her expression: her eyes told me that yes, she was on board, that she trusted me, and we were in it together.

We would ride out these tough times with the promise of better days ahead.

DON'T BLOW IT WITH THE PEOPLE WHO MATTER MOST

I distinctly remember at one point, making the promise to myself: *whatever you do, Brian, don't blow it with your family*. I knew I had it good: my wife was so incredibly patient and would probably have accepted my pushing the limits even further in allowing my work to intrude on our family life. But I also had a growing awareness of how stressful the situation was becoming for all of us. I definitely didn't want to mess things up by overstepping and creating even more friction.

From the beginning, **she had been by my side on this crazy entrepreneur adventure and "in it to win it."** When I asked her to marry me, I made sure she understood what she was getting herself into. I told her it was going to be "fucking crazy." I know: romantic choice of words, right? My proposal actually *was* very romantic—surprise dinner, Al Green's "Love and Happiness" (one of our favorite songs), flowers, ring, the whole nine yards—but it was also very practical in a way that felt true to us. I laid it all out for her: inevitably there would be challenges, problems, issues, stuff I couldn't even anticipate. I wanted her to be 100 percent clear-eyed about what our future would look like, all the ups and downs, twists and turns, triumphs and failures.

Amazingly, she still wanted to be with me. She said yes.

Everyone remembers how they proposed to their spouse. After all, it's one of the biggest days of one's life. But, I also remember another important, highly practical conversation Andrea and I had in our early days about what we wanted for our future. We agreed that, basically, yes, I should *go for it.*

Let's do this thing and chase the dream and make sure we have enough money to support a family.

> As an entrepreneur, it definitely helps to have a spouse or significant other who understands your passion and is "in it to win it" with you—but that doesn't mean you can take their patience for granted.

There was a time early on in our relationship that Andrea and I went to the movies, and I tried to buy tickets—I had no cash on me, and the debit card was declined. So we just got in the car and left. Even though money was not my primary driver as an entrepreneur, at times like this, it became a pretty strong motivator for both of us to succeed and figure out how to get through the rough patches.

Andrea was always very understanding and tolerant. I knew that her personality would allow her to withstand a lot, whether financial struggles or me not being there as much as we wanted. But what I worried about was that she would internalize these pressures and say she was okay until it all blew up.

At a certain point, after the birth of our first child, I decided to make it a rule for myself to be home for dinner four days a week. It became critical to me that I be back by dinner time on those days.

The impetus for this new routine was that things had gotten so out of control that I just knew something had to give. **I had been working 24/7 for months. I felt like a man possessed.** I knew I had to change my environment—be in the house with my family—in order to change my behavior. But if I'm being honest with myself, even when I had been at home over the past months, sometimes I wasn't really home. My mind was not there. I'd be on my phone constantly. Deep down, I knew it wasn't right. I knew that I wanted and needed to be a present and involved father.

But it was more than that, too. It was about me and the kind of life I wanted.

ALIGNING YOUR PROFESSIONAL AND PERSONAL SELF

I had always tried to remind myself that money wouldn't bring happiness. I had once read a famous *New York Times* article about how you need a certain amount of money to not worry about your survival and have your basic necessities taken care of, but beyond that, making a ton of money doesn't actually make you any happier.

This didn't stop me from working relentlessly to achieve what I had set out to do.

It may sound odd, but one thing that always worried me about working so hard was that I would become a boring person—so fixated on building my business that I stopped learning or caring about anything else. This fear was actually related to my marriage as well: specifically, I worried that Andrea would find me less interesting because I didn't have any pursuits beyond what I was doing professionally!

To this day, I have to catch myself sometimes when I'm around her so that I don't just blather nonstop about this or that aspect of the business, or whatever the "work thing" is that I happen to be so excited about at that moment. I guess it's **the blessing and curse of being an entrepreneur.** On the one hand, you don't *want* to shut off your hypomanic brain because what you're thinking about is just so cool. You're so freaking enthusiastic; it's like an adrenaline hit straight to the vein. But you also know that your obsession has to be combined with a dose of caution, or at least an awareness so that it doesn't consume you completely.

And, if you're like me, you know you have to—or at least you try to—reel it back in a bit when you're around other people, so they don't think you're cuckoo. It's the flip side of possessing this intrinsic motivation and *wanting* to put all your energy behind what you're building (not having to be told to do it). All of that stuff is well and good, but the problem is it makes you want to talk about it all the time!

Not all entrepreneurs get self-conscious about this, but I do. This could just be me, but in my case, the issue manifests itself specifically in my worrying about coming across as a boring person or a workaholic.

> As entrepreneurs, often we're so freaking enthusiastic about the thing we're building that we almost can't talk about anything else—it's a blessing and a curse.

Now, I'm going to say something *really* odd. What made me stop and think about whether I was becoming boring was something you'd probably never expect: *food.* The way I was eating. I was so deep in execution-mode at work that I gave no thought whatsoever to food as something pleasurable in itself. I'd find three restaurants I liked and always ordered the same thing. I'd just be in and out.

It gave me pause because I had always *loved* food and had once been passionate about eating out and discovering new dishes and flavors. Who was this person I had become? I wasn't savoring the dining experience at all anymore. That would have required energy, and I wanted to preserve my energy for work. Instead, I had developed this robotic, systematic way of eating that was utterly depressing.

Only now am I rediscovering my love for food, and I am happy to report that it feels great. But even to this day, my old way of thinking crops up now and again. For example, I don't like to spend a lot of time looking at a menu, and the subconscious reason for that, I believe, is that I know it requires brainpower,

CPU, to process all of those menu items. So I just make a quick decision or let my wife decide. It's a weird behavioral adaptation I've developed that I can't seem to shake!

But I digress. My point is that, even though I still cling to my old ways sometimes, I've come back around to savoring the experience of food and eating—and it has been a great way to let my brain rest.

THE IMPORTANCE OF RESPITE

It took time, but gradually, I came to realize the simple truth that **not everything you do as an entrepreneur is as important as you may think it is.** For example, back when I used to stay at Diego's house in Sao Paulo, I would wake up in the morning on Saturdays or Sundays and tell him I was going to the office. To him, it almost felt like an expectation that he should be going too.

"Do you want *me* to go?" he would ask.

"No, dude," I would say, "you do whatever you've got to do on your Sunday. It's all good."

I really meant it. But he had trouble understanding or accepting that I was truly okay with him having a life! Part of this was probably cultural. Americans tend to be more direct and literal in what we say. On the other end of the spectrum, perhaps is Japanese culture, where communication tends to be very discreet. There, I've found that you have to read between the lines and observe not just what people say but how they do or don't act on their words in practice. Brazil is somewhere in the middle. There can sometimes be layers of meaning beyond what is being said, and Diego was likely interpreting my behavior as a passive-aggressive statement of some sort.

But that really wasn't the case at all! I knew how highly motivated he was. That was never an issue. Eventually, he and I became familiar with each other's communication patterns and stopped having these misunderstandings.

But what I wish he could have known, back then, is that far from judging him, I actually *envied* his ability to shut off, to separate and compartmentalize. It was something that I had always struggled with and wouldn't learn for many more years.

Who knew that, of all things, rekindling my love for food would be one of the main inspirations for making these changes?

But it wasn't just that. There were other activities too, like reading books, for example. I used to not read widely across genres. Again, I thought of it as a waste of valuable energy, a distraction from my main purpose. But then I found, to my surprise, that reading something like a Michael Crichton novel felt amazing. It created a kind of separation that I needed and must have been craving.

Shutting off is not antithetical to your ambition as an entrepreneur. In fact, it's often exactly what is needed.

The idea of letting your brain rest is certainly not original to me, but I have seen its power firsthand. Some of my best ideas came when I was on vacation. Some of the best creative moments I've had in terms of how to solve big problems—for example, completely shifting the focus of our business—came in those unlikely periods when I was involved in an activity totally unrelated to my work.

It makes sense when you think about it. Even when you're scuba diving or rock climbing or whatever may float your boat, you don't completely block out the voice in your head that's spinning about work. As an entrepreneur who's building something important and is obsessed with making it succeed, you're always still thinking about the business somewhere in the back of your mind. When you focus your energy outward, deep down, you're still absorbing and processing. But there's a healthy mental break, and often it's just what's needed to get out of your same old thought patterns and come to a new discovery.

My co-founder, Thomas, and I had this experience in the late 2000s, after the real estate crisis. Many of our customers were going out of business. We knew we were in trouble. **If we didn't do something, figure out a way to reinvent ourselves, our business was going to die.** We had to go back to the drawing board.

So we took a little trip, the two of us, to a town in the middle of nowhere in Colombia where they have thermal baths. We slept on bunk beds and spent our days trying to rethink our business. We didn't actually come to the new idea there, but soon after that trip, I went on a vacation to Europe that I had been planning for a while. Coincidentally, Thomas also went on a vacation around the same time. Then, amazingly, we both came back from our respective escapes with a really similar idea. After having beaten our heads against the wall for so long and not coming up with the solution we had hoped for at our earlier getaway, it turned out that letting go and just taking a real vacation was exactly what we needed to unlock our imaginations.

We both returned to work with a realigned way of thinking about the business. Remarkably, my new vision and his were almost completely in-sync. We both saw an opportunity with where we should go and what our reconstructed business should look like.

How cool is that?

In order for us to turn our minds on, we first had to turn our minds off.

TURNING YOUR MIND OFF

Often at night, I literally dream of myself lying there in bed thinking about a problem and how to solve it. It's so weird: it's like I'm wrestling with the concept while I'm sleeping but also seeing myself from the outside as I'm doing it. Then I wake up and, more often than you might expect, have actually solved the problem. It feels good at the moment, like I've accomplished something productive. But it messes with my sleep and is not a healthy practice.

So, to try to turn my mind off, I started listening—every night before I went to sleep—to a song that I find especially soothing: "Chopin's Nocturne Op 9, No. 2." I've actually come to train my brain to associate sleep with the pleasing piano melody. This all started during the period when I was in the middle of executing on the plan Thomas and I had come up with. It was a stressful time, but the familiar tune helped me stop my mind from racing—and then my body, in turn, became trained to relax.

Obviously, that hack, if you will, is very specific to me, and other people will have similar tools of their own. What matters most is not *what* you do but that you keep at it. The habits don't just happen on their own. You have to consciously implement them, in the same way that I forced myself to create boundaries with my time. For example, I made a rule that Sunday would be a day off, a day for my family and me. But I really had to work to create the self-discipline needed to enforce that boundary.

Eventually, I came to realize that carving out time like this wasn't actually a sacrifice to my work productivity at all. **When you're working all the time, on nights and weekends, you're *not* really that productive.** People think they're getting so much done, but they're only going through the motions. It's a matter of quantity over quality. This was a pitfall that my other co-founder, Thomas, saw in himself and tried to rectify. I did too, but not until much later.

Nowadays, I have a number of routines that I cherish, like how Andrea and I have coffee at 4 p.m. every day. It's been a great way for us to just connect and sync up with each other, not only in terms of practical matters but also with our feelings and emotions. But the routine wouldn't have stuck if we hadn't been strict about it.

You have to be kind of religious about these routines at first until they become habitual.

> Healthy habits for turning your mind off and routines for setting boundaries with your time don't just happen on their own—you have to consciously implement them.

Putting in place these new behaviors and techniques to allow myself to shut off has been hugely beneficial to me and my overall well-being in recent months and years. But I'd be lying if I said that I have it all figured out now. In fact, in 2019, I had another panic attack. The stress and anxiety had been building up in me from a combination of overworking and flying around to different countries trying to raise capital.

This was also coming off the heels of a very stressful 2018 when we had to deal with the growing pains of operating as a merged company after Viva Real joined forces with its competitor, ZAP. It was a rocky year: the business wasn't growing, and one of our key people was being lured to another company. As for the latter development, ultimately this person stayed, but he came scarily close to leaving, which would have been very painful indeed as we were in the midst of merging two technology companies, and he was our head of technology!

Meanwhile, we were still going through the worst of the merger pains, which resulted in flat/negative growth through the first half of 2018—making it very difficult and stressful for me to be out there trying to raise capital for the business.

All in all, it felt like everything had been spiraling out of control through 2018, and even though a sense of hope had been restored with the exciting offer in May 2019—the $600–$700 million for Grupo ZAP Viva Real that I talked about in the book's opening pages—I still had a lingering pain like a wound that hadn't fully healed.

Then, it began to seem like the deal was in jeopardy, and the stress put me over the edge. What triggered the panic attack wasn't so much the consequences for *me* if the deal fell apart, but I knew that key people in the company needed money—their shares didn't have any liquidity—and I felt responsible. There were kids' educations to pay for. My best friend, James, who had taken a bet on me early on, needed money. And my co-founder Diego was desperate to help his father recover financially after a bogus legal ordeal where Diego's dad had been the real victim but wound up in crippling debt. I tried to put together a secondary transaction, but it was blocked by the board. The cumulative effect of all these stressful circumstances was too much to bear.

If you've ever experienced a panic attack, you know how traumatic it is. You think you're dying. Your brain is literally sending the message: *you are dying.* But when you come out the other side, you can sometimes gain a new perspective on what was stressing you out in the first place.

For me, the panic attack was a learning experience around how to deal with the inherent anxiety of these situations. In particular, it made me realize how important it is for me to stay healthy—both physically and mentally.

Managing your health and psychology as a founder or entrepreneur of an ambitious organization that's trying to go after a big opportunity and make a massive impact, especially if you're raising capital, is no small feat. From the stress and anxiety discussed in chapter one to the tremendous toll it can take on your personal life (like we've explored in this chapter), you're definitely going to need strength and fortitude that you've probably never called upon and don't even know you possess.

To succeed in this journey of founding, scaling, and raising venture capital in Latin America, you're going to face many obstacles. Some of them will even be existential threats.

I have deliberately structured my book so that you can first learn here, in Part One, about the broadest types of challenges faced by leaders and CEOs. Now you will have a sturdy foundation for the chapters in Part Two and Three about the nuts and bolts of building and raising funds for businesses in Latin America.

But before we get to all that, I want to look at one of the most widespread and difficult issues you see in the entrepreneurial world and one that I have dealt with plenty of times myself, for better or worse.

In chapter three, we delve into the challenges of managing relationships with co-founders.

THE CO-FOUNDER RELATIONSHIP

Ideally, startups will have one technical co-founder and one who's more business/sales-oriented—with the latter often (not always) taking the role of CEO (titles are largely meaningless when you're starting out anyway). Your co-founder is the person in the trenches with you who'll pick you up when you're knee-deep in shit and pull you out. But there are many challenges that come with this relationship, and co-founder disputes are, in fact, the number one early startup killer. Not surprisingly, money is one of the thorniest issues, from compensation to misalignment of equity—and co-founders must vest their shares right from the beginning. But there are also challenges around shifting roles and responsibilities, with co-founders often feeling threatened by new hires. Another co-founder bone of contention has to do with who gets credit and recognition for the company's successes. Success will often mask co-founder problems, which is why Brian calls upon readers to stay vigilant—to obsess over communication, acknowledging and respecting people's different styles—so that resentments don't fester. Ultimately, says the author, trust is the most important ingredient between co-founders.

First things first: *you need a co-founder.* Don't even think about trying to get by without one; it's simply too hard to go it alone. You absolutely need that person who will always have your back, and chip in without hesitation no matter what you need.

Ideally, you and your co-founder (or co-founders) should have a *balance* of skills and abilities to offset and support each other in a complementary way. This is especially important for tech companies. The best co-founder relationships I've seen are those where one founder is more technical- or product-oriented, and the other is more business- or sales-oriented (the fundraiser who's managing the money).

I get asked a lot of times, "Who should be the CEO, you or your co-founder?" My response: titles are mostly bullshit in the early days anyway. When you're just starting out, you and your co-founder are doing *everything*. Your company is still small, and you don't have any employees yet (or if you do, it's probably just a few).

As you build your team, you *will* want to define what roles people have. There can still be plenty of improvisation, but you don't want your whole team to get sucked into a hard task, like fundraising. Titles *do* help to carve out the different roles and responsibilities internally. And if you pick your co-founders well, the CEO question will be taken care of by complementary skills. With Thomas and me, it wasn't entirely clear-cut. But when we launched our business, the natural sorting was that I took care of sales, marketing, B2B marketing, business development, and all customer-facing roles, and he assumed product engineering, design, and search engine marketing. We did recruiting together (recruiting is a symbiotic relationship: you help each other recruit).

I don't even think we ever had an explicit conversation about who should be CEO. It just became apparent. When we went out and talked to investors, I led the conversations.

When you're starting or running a business, you have to leave your ego at the door. You do what's best for the company. Whoever is more comfortable being an external person—interfacing with clients, talking to journalists, getting on stage and presenting, and pitching your idea—should be the CEO. Thomas didn't like doing any of those things, so it was only natural that I would step into the role of CEO.

If you're the person responsible for sales—whose job it is to always be thinking about the money—you should be CEO.

Again, this distinction is not always clear when a startup is still in its infancy, but as you and your co-founder evolve into your natural roles, whichever one of you owns sales, fundraising, and money matters should assume the mantle of CEO.

> The number one job of the CEO is to make sure the business doesn't run out of money.

Does this natural sorting of roles and responsibilities mean that founders should never challenge themselves to develop new muscles? I wouldn't go that far, but for the most part, I've always believed the smart move *is to double-down* on your strengths and find other people to supplement where you have weaknesses.

This is especially true in a startup where speed is the number-one advantage. I once heard a memorable analogy about this from General Partner Gigi Levy of NFX. Monashees Capital had organized a trip to Tel Aviv, Israel, with a group of sixty founders from Brazil, and it was there that Gigi gave the following explanation for why the race belongs to the swift. "Think about it like this," he said. "If you're playing chess and can move twice for every single move made by your opponent, even you can beat a grandmaster."

You have to be fast in this startup game, and that's also why I don't recommend ever having *two* CEOs. Some people are drawn to this idea of *co-CEOs*, and I know people who have made it work, like my friends Mate Pencz and Florian Hagenbuch, founders of Loft and Canary. And of course, you have the legendary entrepreneurs and investors—now located in the Silicon Valley but with deep experience in Latin America—Meyer Malka (aka Micky) and Wences Casares. (Full disclosure: Micky and Wences are also investors in my company.) But I've also seen this strategy explode.

Not only does sharing the CEO role make things harder when you have investors, in my opinion, it sends a weird message to your team. Say a team member needs feedback from leadership on this or that business matter. If there's any difference of opinion among the two CEOs, it creates a delay—and again, **anything that slows down decision-making in a startup is the kiss of death**.

It's especially important for your investors, and your team, to always know who is responsible for making major financial decisions about the business.

Which brings us to one of the most important and thorny issues in the co-founder relationship: money.

MONEY MATTERS AMONG CO-FOUNDERS

The very first thing you need to do when you start your company with your co-founder is **vest your shares**. What do I mean by that? Say you and your co-founder each own 45 percent of the company, with the remaining 10 percent in an option pool for recruiting executives. When you vest your shares, it means you and your co-founder don't actually own that 45 percent from the beginning. Rather, you earn it over time. The logic behind this arrangement is that he or she might not work out— more often than not, there *are* problems with co-founders—and you have to protect yourself.

What are all the things that can go wrong? Lots! Maybe you realize soon after starting the company that the responsibilities are just too much for the person. Maybe some unexpected event in their lives makes it impossible for them to continue. Or maybe they've got conflicting ideas, and these different visions turn out to be irreconcilable. The last thing you want is to find yourself two years in, and 30–40 percent of the company's equity is tied-up with a co-founder who isn't adding any value. It may seem obvious, but I've seen it happen plenty of times—and not only is it ugly, but it makes you a highly unattractive target for investment.

> Co-founder disputes are the number one early startup killer.

Misalignment of equity is something that can also cause a rift between co-founders. You see this constantly in startups: one person puts in a lot more money than the other, and it creates an uneasy dynamic.

That said, you should probably avoid a 50/50 partnership. The problem with 50/50 equity is that it can lead to an awkward deadlock when there are difficult decisions that have to be made one way or another. Knowing that there is one person responsible ultimately for making the call eases the burden for all involved. Obviously, this person should be a great listener and have an effective process and style for taking everyone's input into consideration. But in order to reach better and faster outcomes, there needs to be that one co-founder who is the official decider. (This usually happens over time anyway because, more often than not, one of the co-founders has outsized experience or has put in much more money.)

Thankfully, Thomas and I never had an issue with equity. As you know by now, I had two co-founders at Viva Real. Thomas was there at the beginning. Diego came on when we entered into Brazil after Thomas and I had already been running the company for two years.

Thomas and I were pretty much equal equity partners. I had slightly more equity than him because I put some of my own money in. But we never got into any conflicts over it.

Nor did we ever fight over salaries. Just like with equity, **compensation (or who gets paid what) can create problems among co-founders**. As a founder, it is important in general to keep your salary low: when you're deciding on compensation for yourself, you are also setting a bar for the rest of the organization. But in terms of co-founder disputes, typically what happens is that at some point, the CEO starts to make more money than the other founders—and this was true for me. In the beginning, neither Thomas nor I took salaries at all. But eventually, when we started scaling and raising more capital, I ended up making more money than him.

It didn't ruffle Thomas. His personality was just so humble that he took a devil-may-care attitude of *whatever, you can make more money than me, I don't mind.*

When Diego, our other co-founder, came on, we started him with a small salary and also gave him equity—but of course, this equity was less than ours because he was joining the company later.

Over the coming years, some issues *did* emerge in Diego's and my co-founder relationship, and I made some mistakes there, which I will talk about throughout this chapter.

These co-founder challenges I experienced with Diego weren't so much about equity or compensation (there *was* a misunderstanding later on where he thought he had a lower percentage of equity than he really did—but we cleared it up!).

Rather, the problems had to do with another very common bone of contention among co-founders: shifting roles and responsibilities.

ROLES AND RESPONSIBILITIES FOR CO-FOUNDERS

When you grow to a certain level as a company beyond the initial stage where people are wearing lots of different hats, you start to have to specialize. That's hard for a lot of founders because they're used to tackling all these responsibilities and filling all these roles *themselves*. Now they have to choose. What is their specific thing going to be?

Finding the right specialty for co-founders can be fraught. Say, for example, you have someone who is highly gifted when it comes to the technical side of the company. As the business grows, what is going to happen to them? Either they can continue to focus on the tech and not try to be a people manager or they can scale up and take on the new people-managing responsibilities. Either way, there is a lot of potential for the person to get offended.

Sure, there are other reasons for co-founder drama, like not seeing eye-to-eye in general about where the company should be focused—but from my perspective, **clarity of roles** is one of the biggest, if not *the* biggest challenge in co-founder relationships. I have seen many partnerships blow up over this as the company scales. It isn't usually a problem in the beginning because in an early-stage startup, there is so much to do that everyone stays busy, and your roles are less focused.

As a company grows, by definition, co-founders have to let go and delegate responsibilities to others. But that can be difficult for a lot of people. Sometimes co-founders won't have the right skillset as the company evolves or, in the worst of scenarios, will feel threatened by new hires and get upset.

I understand why someone might feel this way. But it's how businesses work. In fact, as a co-founder, you should *want* to make yourself replaceable, at least in terms of certain tasks and aspects of the business. This means you can focus on other things. It's a good sign: it shows that your people are executing, and you're succeeding in what you're trying to build.

But the reality is that some co-founders struggle with making room for the new hires. At a certain point at Viva Real, I brought on a bunch of new executives, and it created friction with Diego. He didn't make enough room for the people coming in. But instead of talking to him directly about it like I should have—and having the courage to really address his concerns head-on and explain what I needed from him—I sought the easy way out. I wanted to avoid conflict, so I tried to have my cake and eat it too.

Looking back now, I can see that there were some style differences at play with the new folks I brought on. They had a different approach to work: they were focused exclusively on results and probably didn't value the people portion of the business as much as Diego and I did. They were hard-charging and admittedly lacked some sensibilities around people's feelings. Diego felt protective of the strong cultural roots we had built, and rightfully so. There were indeed some negative aspects to the new way of doing things that came along with the new hires, but back then, I didn't see it quite as negatively as Diego did.

The style differences caused a lot of tension, and I tried my hardest to correct the imbalance. But maybe I didn't go about it the right way. Because Diego wasn't making room for the new hires, I took it upon myself to make room for them. I didn't want to lose Diego. After all, he was really *good*. There was a reason I had brought him on in the first place. So I ended up trying to create something *for* him, i.e., new roles adapted around him.

That was a mistake. **You should never create a role around a person; you should always create it around the needs of your business.** It was one of many mistakes that I made as a first-time CEO. But I did what I thought would work so that Diego, who added great value to the company, could stay on.

I didn't know exactly what his role should be, so we tried on a lot of different things. At one point, he took over HR and hated that. Then, he took over B2B marketing and *was* good at that. But we ended up hiring someone else to focus exclusively on B2B marketing, which pushed him out of the seat.

It's a classic startup trajectory: at the beginning, you have lots of generalists, but as the company grows, you can really only have one generalist, which is the CEO. Understandably, it makes it hard for the other co-founders. Either they get pushed out, or they really embrace a specific role.

Thomas had this issue too, but with him, it wasn't as bad. As mentioned earlier, on any founding team, you need someone who's very technical. If it's not your co-founder, it's someone on the founding team who you hire early in a product-centric company like ours. Thomas was good at product, but he wasn't super technical. He wasn't an engineer. So we never really had a CTO. We always struggled with that. Thomas ended up having to be the CTO even though he did not code.

Frankly, we always had a bit of weakness there because Thomas didn't have a background in deep engineering. In a way, we set ourselves up for failure and were never able to fully fill that gap in the early days. We had a couple of people we brought on at the beginning, but none of them were the true engineering leaders we needed to oversee everything. Thomas and I both agreed that if we were to launch another startup, we would have a strong CTO from day one.

I'm not exactly sure what could have been done differently to have avoided this issue with Thomas. It all worked itself out in the end. But I *do* know that with Diego, my inclination to avoid conflict was the wrong call. Sadly, it wasn't the only mistake I made with him. Despite my good intentions, I also failed to fully anticipate the inevitable potential for resentment over who was getting all the credit and recognition for our successes.

WHO GETS CREDIT AMONG CO-FOUNDERS

I never thought of myself as Diego's boss, but I realized later that he thought of me that way. Maybe I *should* have seen myself as his boss, but I was just so focused on making the business the best it could be. I realize this may sound naïve, but I genuinely didn't look at what we were building together in those terms of a traditional business hierarchy.

The reason Thomas and I had brought Diego on in the first place was that we needed him to run the Brazilian market. Remember: when we first started in Brazil, we were still focused on many different markets. Diego was going to be the country manager for one of those markets.

It soon became clear, however, that Brazil was our biggest opportunity. I moved there and became CEO. That alone was not an issue with Diego. I had given him a heads-up when he joined the team that eventually we would be finding a CEO. At the time, I didn't know that the person was going to be me. But given that Diego didn't have a lot of experience, I wanted to set the stage right off the bat that it wasn't going to be him.

Unlike Thomas, Diego was more of a generalist—same as me. His background was in business administration. And I actually learned a lot from him about how to be a good manager since I had held very few management roles myself up to that point. Nonetheless, the fact that Diego was a generalist became an issue, as we've already talked about. As the company grew, and we hired more specialists, we struggled to figure out what his niche in the company would be. But there was more to the co-founder problems between the two of us than just that.

After I moved to Brazil as CEO there, we started to raise a lot more money and get a lot of PR. I found myself doing more and more interviews. In retrospect, there were times when I probably got a little too high on myself, seeing my face on the front cover of the newspaper, and so on. I tried really hard not to fall into that trap, not let myself go on an ego trip, but I can't 100 percent say I never succumbed to it.

What I *can* say is that, when talking to journalists, I tried as often as I could to plug my co-founders. I didn't want Thomas and Diego to always have to see me at the center of every story. I wanted to give them shine too. They poured as much energy into the business day in and day out as I did. They knew that. I knew that. I wanted everyone to know that. But when you're talking to a journalist, you only have so much control over what they write.

With Thomas, I'm pretty confident there was little resentment. But with Diego, I know there was—and I take responsibility for that. I should have been more up front with him and talked about it more from the beginning to nip any potential bad feelings in the bud. I should have seen it coming that my increased visibility would eventually become a problem, and I should have been more proactive about not letting it get out of control.

Looking back now, I can see how it must have stung. It wasn't even Diego himself so much, but the pressure he felt from outside. His family would see me in the newspaper and ask, "Why is it always Brian? Why aren't you in the mix?" Understandably, this created a weird dynamic for him.

Knowing what I know now, I would have handled everything a little differently. But even back then, I believed in the same general principle I do today, which is that you should **always try to prop your people up**—and if you engage them in a way that makes them feel important, they will also feel more supported.

I understood, both then and now, the importance of making people feel involved and connected with what they're doing as a way of building greater engagement. I think this is just good general practice in any business.

Where I fell short was that I underestimated the gap between what I was *trying* to do—raise up my people—and the *reality* of how my actions would be perceived by those same individuals.

Have conversations early and often to check in on the emotional temperature of your co-founders.

Admittedly, even in my trying to big up Diego and Thomas, this wasn't an altogether egoless approach on my part: yes, it was for the greater benefit of the business and the success of what we all shared and built together, but, of course, the company's success also benefited me personally.

Moreover, I knew that ultimately it would help us in the investors' eyes to be perceived—accurately—as an extraordinary collective, at least in terms of the founding team and all the executives. I knew there was an instant value attachment to that. It was a good look for us *all* to be seen in a great light by investors, the media, and the whole ecosystem because it added to the company's overall credibility and value.

The truth is: we *were* pretty amazing together. Working so

closely with one another, we developed a kind of rhythm and a shorthand that only happens when you're spending tons of time with a person. Our communication as co-founders wasn't perfect, as we've seen in my missteps with Diego, but for the most part, we all came to understand and respect one another's distinct styles of communicating. We learned through trial and error to adapt and tweak our ways of interacting toward whatever was needed so that we could best work together and solve any problems at hand.

THE IMPORTANCE OF HEALTHY COMMUNICATION WITH CO-FOUNDERS

As an entrepreneur, you must **always be obsessing about communication**. It's the foundation of everything: without it, the building will come crumbling down.

The challenge is that different people can have completely different styles of communication. Thomas, for example, was unquestionably a C on the DISC profile model. If you're not familiar with DISC, it's a personality test that classifies people into four different types. There's D for dominant, I for influencer, S for service-oriented, and C for critical thinker. (If you want to find your own DISC profile, go to crystalknows.com.)

Thomas was and is a highly critical thinker. He would always send me these super long emails. I would read the email and then call him up and talk about it. That was the way we communicated: him in writing and me verbally.

He was the same way when it came to product and engineering. Something would come up and I'd just go over to talk to him. But he wasn't having it. He'd tell me straight-out: "I'm locked in right now. I'm working on something. You're breaking my flow." I had to gradually figure out the best way to communicate with him, such as setting aside a time rather than just coming at him willy-nilly.

> What are the different communication styles among you and your co-founders? How are you navigating and respecting these differences?

I've often thought about how the co-founder relationship is like a marriage. Thomas and I developed routines—similar to my 4 p.m. coffee with Andrea—where we'd go on daily walks together around the park, just doing a loop and letting the conversation flow, shooting the shit about everything he and I happened to have on our minds.

Now, of course, my routines with my wife are a little bit different because, well, she's my wife. But there are definitely similarities, and, as I learned with Thomas and Diego, a good co-founder relationship, like a good marriage, is *not* one where you never argue or fight. It's all about *how* you express your disagreements.

Like with a spouse, **trust is at the very foundation of the co-founder relationship**. If you don't have trust, you're done. This is especially true with co-founders, but it's good advice across the board and something you should try to develop with your whole team. This trust is built through alignment in values and is proven with actions. To have trust is to be sure that your co-founders possess certain values that will drive their actions. And the reason you are sure is that you have seen them demonstrate those values with actions over an extended period of time.

I learned a lot about trust from the framework for teamwork

called the Five Behaviors of a Cohesive Team Model. Trust is the base of the pyramid. There are five layers. Once there is trust, this allows for Conflict (the next layer up) because now you have enough of a foundation of goodwill to disagree, sometimes fiercely. Next, by engaging in that conflict, you start to create Commitment to each other. And once you're able to make a Commitment, you can have Accountability—which is what leads, finally, to Results.

The Five Behaviors of a Cohesive Team™ Model

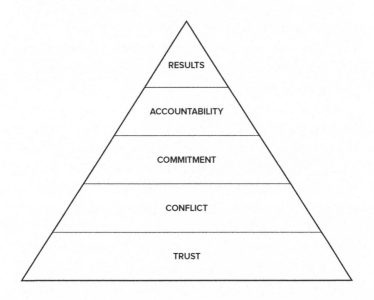

RESULTS

ACCOUNTABILITY

COMMITMENT

CONFLICT

TRUST

One important element that's not covered in that framework, however, is *gratitude*—expressing thanks and appreciation to your co-founder for everything they do and for your partnership as a whole, including all the speed bumps along the way and the valuable lessons learned.

Like in a marriage, **sometimes you've got to take the time with**

your co-founders to just connect and sync-up. One of the ways that Thomas and I, in particular, managed to stay close through the course of our relationship is that we both went through personal struggles during those years. Thomas had two divorces. Andrea and I had the issue of not being able to get pregnant, her being in the US, and all the struggles with not being close together. Both of us had periods of mild depression.

Through it all, you have to always maintain your admiration for the person as a human being—as well as for their unique skills and value they add to the company. I sincerely felt this way about both Thomas and Diego. They are both awesome.

> You've got to be there for your co-founders in their personal struggles. The whole reason you're in this together is to pick each other up.

When all is said and done, conflicts will inevitably emerge between you and your co-founders, and that's fine. In fact, I think good partnerships often thrive on conflict. As long as you remember the underlying intentions—going back to the fundamental mission of what you're trying to build together and why you're building it—your disagreements as co-founders can sharpen your strategy and help you level-up.

The problem is when you're immovable in your thinking. As much as Thomas and I argued over the years, he was always able to enhance my ideas by challenging them—and we always got to a better place after arguing.

In short, **as long as you're enhancing each other and not being combative in a damaging way, then co-founder conflict can be a very good and positive force in startups.**

SUCCESS MASKS CO-FOUNDER PROBLEMS

These communication issues are usually fixable. But if your co-founder is, for whatever reason, not living up to their end of the bargain—as outlined in the agreement regarding their vested equity—or it becomes clear they're not in the right role, it's obviously better to cut ties sooner rather than later. Usually, what happens in these scenarios is that you both kind of realize it.

Ironically, the more challenging situation is when, despite co-founder problems, the business becomes really successful. Success will mask co-founder problems and cause you to avoid the kind of healthy, necessary conflict that is so important in a startup.

Of course, the opposite is also true: when your business *isn't* going as well, you tend to have greater co-founder conflict.

What's most important is that even when you're in the middle of a conflict, remember that it's not always going to feel as serious as it does at that moment. Keep things in perspective. With both Thomas and Diego, apart from a few blow-ups, we never really got all that upset with one another. And when we did have those fights, we made sure to patch it up and often took the opportunity to acknowledge our gratitude. Thomas and I would say things like: "Dude, what an amazing partnership we've had for a whole decade now."

> Embrace co-founder conflict, but make sure you're fighting fair. If the conflict runs the risk of getting out of control, establish boundaries.

When Thomas ended up leaving the company in 2015, he told me, "I want to leave. I'm tired. I don't want to do this anymore." It was the one blowout we ever had. He told me he never wanted to work with me again, and I told him I should have fired his ass!

The investors weren't thrilled with the news that he was leaving, and I definitely felt hurt and abandoned. Yes, it happens, especially in bigger companies. When you have a team of 200 people, all with different responsibilities like we did at that point, the co-founder role that Thomas had occupied becomes somewhat less important (certainly less critical than it would have been early on). Nonetheless, there was a big gap in part of the business as a result of his absence.

Jumping ahead, I stepped down myself a year later in 2016, and when I did, I actually helped convince Thomas to come back to the company for a year, which was really helpful. At the time, we had a problem involving a very important part of our business. I knew Thomas was the best person to solve it, and he came in and did just that—along with Lucas, my successor as CEO (they worked on it together).

Looking back now on all of it, I just think: what an amazing journey.

I am so grateful to both of my co-founders.

I've also learned a lot since those days from the co-founder mistakes I made. I recognize that structural obstacles made it hard for both Thomas and Diego to maintain relevance in the business. **How do you maintain relevance if you're not the CEO?** It's not easy. But what I would advise for people in that position is to develop a strong, specific skillset that's fundamental to the business, a critical role that they can really own.

Often, a technical co-founder will be very good at execution but not have the right skillset to manage an engineering team. There's something called a Y career path that you see a lot of in product engineering, where you go one of two routes: stay on as an individual contributor building the code or go into management. But even with the latter, usually people have to *learn* how to manage teams. It makes sense: most co-founders are pretty green in their overall careers. If it's their first company, obviously they've never had the experience of scaling a team. So they don't know what it's like to build out all the processes. But those skills can be learned.

This wasn't the path for Diego, of course. He was a generalist, not a technical co-founder. But I could have done a better job communicating with him about the new path he was going to need to carve for himself as the company grew. I landed too much on the side of avoiding conflict rather than speaking hard truths.

As you've seen over the course of this chapter, to a certain degree, co-founder conflicts just go with the territory—and can be for the best.

In my case, I am happy to report that all three of us are cool with each other these days, which is a big part of why I'm comfortable sharing these stories in my book, and in fact, I believe our relationships are all the better now not in spite of, but *because of* our blow-ups.

FOUNDING AND SCALING YOUR COMPANY

THE VALUE OF VIRTUES

The best companies are purpose-driven, inspired by an impulse to solve a real problem in the world. This was certainly true for Brian; he knew that he and his co-founders were onto something promising with their real estate business because he understood the pain point personally as a consumer. With purpose-driven businesses, often, the intrinsic motivator (beyond money) is a specific social mission, and in a way, this is true of almost every business in Latin America because they are creating jobs and contributing to a developing economy. Founders must go beyond just establishing their purpose; however, the next step is for them to translate their "why" into a series of cultural principles or virtues. Often referred to as core values, Brian prefers the word "virtues" because it implies action, not just talk. He encourages readers to spell out your virtues right from the get-go, so that initial hires know exactly what the company stands for culturally. The baseline DNA of any organization emanates from its founders, and it's essential that you live the company culture in your own behavior. Here, Brian shows exactly how to identify the virtues that are meaningful and authentic to you—and how to then operationalize them at scale.

Before building my business in real estate and moving to Colombia, I had pretty much been living out of my car, traveling through Mexico and Central America. It was an amazing adventure. But when I got to Colombia, where I was visiting Andrea, and decided to extend my stay, I needed a real place to live.

Initially, I shacked up in a crappy motel in a pretty sketchy part of Bogota. You have to understand that "motel" in Colombia is the same concept as it is in Brazil. I thought it was more like a Motel 6 or Super 8 in the States, just a lower-end hotel. Essentially, it's a place you rent by the hour. But I didn't know that at the time. It was just the cheapest thing I could find.

Soon after I arrived, I went out with Andrea and her family. At this point, we had already been in a long-distance relationship for nine months (and had dated for five months before that in San Diego). I had come to Colombia to visit her and see if the relationship would go anywhere. So, when she asked me to join her family for a night out, it felt like a big deal. Her family are high-society people, and we got all dressed up to go to a show at a really beautiful theatre in a fancy part of the city.

This is probably TMI, but I'm going to tell you anyway. Ever since arriving in Colombia, I'd been subsisting almost exclusively on a cheap diet of street food. My insides weren't used to fine dining, so when we got to the theatre after our nice meal, I was already experiencing some severe, shall we say, gastrointestinal problems.

I had borrowed my (now) father-in-law's jacket and, even though it was warm in the theatre, I kept it on to cover myself (and whatever my bad stomach was doing). Intermission couldn't come soon enough—I was dying inside. It didn't help that the performance was so quiet and serious. It was a show by a Korean theatre company featuring a man slowly shoveling sand and building it into a kind of intricately patterned spiral structure. I am not shitting you: that was the whole "plot."

You could have heard a pin drop. When we finally got out of there, I was ready to burst.

After barely making it through the night without totally embarrassing myself in front of Andrea's family, I agreed to let them drive me back home. Bad move. "Where are you staying?" they asked. When I told them the address, they responded with, "Oh, that's not a very nice area."

It got worse. They dropped me off at what was clearly a motel and proceeded, I would later learn, to scold Andrea. "You have to get him out of there," they told her. "That's a terrible place for him to stay!"

I knew I needed to find a better apartment if I was going to stay in Colombia. So I picked up the newspaper to see what I could find in the classifieds (there wasn't much information online in those days). One ad looked promising, so I called up and spoke to a real estate agent who said, "Oh, I've got the perfect property for you." We met up at a café, where he opened his briefcase and pulled out a piece of paper with fifteen property listings. "The place you're looking for is definitely on this list," he said.

"Great," I responded. "Let's go check them out."

But then he wagged his finger. "No, no, that will be 20,000 pesos." It wasn't a lot of money, only about $10 at the time. But that was about the same amount I had been paying per night to stay at the motel!

Really, I was grumpy that the guy was charging me at all—and for nothing more than access to the information. But then I thought about the crappy motel where I had been staying. I gave him the money, but the day turned out to be a total waste. The first place I saw was already rented. The second was too big. The third was too expensive. I came away empty-handed.

There's got to be a better way, I thought to myself.

Even though I struck out that day, it turned out to be a blessing in disguise because **my frustration with the process was what inspired my business.** I wanted to build a central repository for real estate information and inventory so that customers could see all their options at once.

I understood the pain point I was trying to solve because I had experienced it myself. When I'd been looking for a place, it was impossible to even know what was available. There was no access to centralized, consolidated information about real estate properties. The consumer was totally disempowered.

I wanted to change that. I wanted to make the inventory information available to everyone—for free.

And that's exactly what my co-founders and I did. We built a massive platform that now has fifty million visits a month in Brazil from people looking for real estate. We also have thousands of advertisers, real estate companies, and others, who put their listings on our site—literally millions of properties, all across the country.

"I understood the pain point I was trying to solve because I had experienced it myself."

I tell this story about the genesis of my company because it speaks to the importance of **purpose**. The best companies are purpose-driven, inspired by an impulse to solve a real problem in the world. This was certainly the case with Viva Real, and I knew we were on to something because I understood the pain point as a consumer.

But after achieving our goal of solving the problem and creating the central repository for real estate information, I realized there was another related problem, which was that the service itself, the customer experience with agents, was frankly terrible for the most part (with the exception of a handful of companies). We hadn't innovated enough, which left an opening and opportunity for someone else: QuintoAndar came in and built a verticalized solution where they handled the whole process of listing the property, servicing the rental, and even offering an insurance product.

I actually ended up investing in Quinto, and I regard Gabriel Braga and Andre Penha as some of the best founders in Brazil. I did receive some criticism for making the investment. Initially, we weren't direct competitors, but as both companies matured, there became more overlap. My mentality was that Viva Real couldn't own the entire ecosystem and that the Quinto founders were bound for success with or without my investment. I learned a lot from them over the years. It also turned out to be (as of this writing) my single best angel investment. But the reason I was able to recognize its value in the first place was that, again, I understood the pain point. It was the same sense of recognition I felt when I had first built Viva Real.

FROM PAIN POINTS TO PURPOSE

Not every single business has to have direct, intimate experience with its customers' pain points, but I do think it's massively validating as a founder when you've personally felt the pain. You are just that much more motivated to solve the problem.

For example, take Nubank's founder and CEO David Vélez, who started the company in 2013 based on the idea of giving people more control over their financial lives. Fast forward seven years, and, as I am writing this book, David's small startup is now in seventh-round Series F funding and has become the largest digital bank in the world! (The capital he raised from prominent investor TCV put the valuation at $10 billion USD.) The whole premise for his business was born out of personal frustration around the banking experience in Brazil: when you go into a bank in that part of the world, because security is such an issue, you have to take out all your belongings, like in an airport. There are armed guards, and you're treated pretty much like a criminal. It's an ordeal just to open an account.

Vélez was fed up with that unpleasant routine and wanted to build something that would solve the problem by moving the banking experience out of the branch and onto the internet. Of course, online banking is quite common already in the US and other parts of the world—and nowadays, it is pretty advanced in Brazil too. But the real innovation that Vélez brought was that his company, Nubank, wasn't burdened by the fixed cost of having branches all across the country. David puts it best, "We are a tech company that happens to be in the financial services business whereas other banks are financial services companies that use technology." This distinction may seem small, but it's one of the main reasons David and his team have been able to create so much value.

Nubank (which started out in Brazil and is now set to take on banks through the entire region) was a pioneer in *so many ways* and is still one of the most innovative companies globally. But it all began with its founder trying to solve a personal problem.

Whatever type of business you're trying to build, you're more likely to come up with a great idea when it's a personal pain point you're trying to solve. But you also have to make sure that what you're trying to achieve is, in fact, a real solution, not just a band-aid—a **pain killer, not a vitamin.**

When it comes to the problem you and your business are setting out to address, are you providing the kind of pill that people are really craving—to help take away, at long last, their persistent pain and aches? Or is your medicine just supplemental? In a lot of cases, founders mistake the two. They think they're solving a deep pain, but in reality, they're just handing out some Vitamin C.

Yes, to be a purpose-driven business means you're motivated by having experienced something that really bothered you, that you feel is unfair or should be different—and you want to make it so that other people don't have to suffer in the same way. But there's more to it than that. Building a business with purpose is about looking at the problem and seeing into the future. It's about asking yourself: how does the world exist today, and how will it be made better tomorrow because of your solution? And what will this new reality look like once you've solved the problem? How will people be happier?

Building a business with purpose is about looking at the problem and seeing the future.

This is what I mean when I talk about needing an intrinsic motivator. Again, it's okay to want money, but the reality is: if you're just in it to become wealthy, you're not going to have the fuel to fight your way through all the friction and craziness that lie ahead. Of course, money is still important. These aren't nonprofits we're talking about. But having an intrinsic motivator makes it that much more likely you'll be able to withstand the severe ups and downs of this wild ride of building a business.

Take, for example, a company I invested in called LiftIt—a Colombian company that has now expanded to not only Brazil but also Mexico, Ecuador, and Chile. It was founded by Brian York. Brian was born in Colombia but adopted at only two weeks old and brought to the United States. He grew up in Boston, not speaking any Spanish, but at a certain point decided he wanted to go back to search for his birth mother. Then, while in Colombia, he saw a business opportunity. He noticed that a lot of people owned their own trucks but worked for big truck companies. There was a huge demand for deliveries. What if— he wondered—all these truck drivers could be consolidated under a single platform?

The premise of his startup was to eliminate the middle man (the big truck companies), and empower the drivers, who ended up with more customers and better margins because they were now able to source their business directly. Ultimately, these same drivers make lots more money and are able to better provide for their families. This meant everything to the founder. It was a way to give back to the country where he was born—which served as a hugely compelling intrinsic motivator for him.

I also invested in another Colombian business (also now expanding internationally) called Chiper, that's based on a similar idea. Throughout Latin America, there are millions of mom-and-pop retail stores run by micro-entrepreneurs—and people have long been predicting that these local community stores are eventually going to be put out of business by the corporate big-box retailers. So, to address this problem, Chiper created a platform that gave these small shop owners the technologies and tools to compete in this challenging marketplace. Chiper did this by unlocking the potential of e-commerce for the small retailers, but also by *uniting* them, which allowed them to buy in volume, thereby increasing their bargaining power.

All in all, Chiper has helped these entrepreneurs fight back against mega-corporations and *win*—not just in terms of great service but also competitive pricing. In the process, they have also changed buyer habits across the region! Every one of these hyperlocal storefronts—hundreds of thousands of them throughout Latin America—is now a node for connecting consumers with a dizzying range of new options and opportunities.

Crucially, this arrangement benefits not just the store owners but also the customers. Yes, by helping to reduce the cost of acquiring the products, Chiper creates higher margins for the shops. But then the stores also pass along part of those savings to consumers, creating lower prices and motivating people to shop local rather than at, say, Walmart.

For many purpose-driven businesses, the intrinsic motivator is a social mission.

To some degree, almost every business in Latin America has a social mission element to it in the sense that the economy is still in development. So, just by building a business, you're able to provide salaries for families to help put their kids through school and create positive cycles.

Certainly, I feel proud of the fact that at Viva Real we created 1000 jobs in Brazil. But that came later. At the beginning, of course, it was just me and Thomas. We talked about what kind of company we were trying to build and why we were building it. But it wasn't until two years in that we actually sat down and tried to capture in writing the *virtues* that would come to define our culture.

TRANSLATING YOUR *WHY* INTO YOUR VIRTUES

What do I mean by virtues?

I use the word intentionally, and in contrast to the more common business term *values*, to emphasize that these are more than just aspirational goals. According to Jack Krupansky, "Virtues are *lived* values, values *in action*, values which are achieved on a dependably regular basis." Too many companies talk a big game about their values when it's really just lip service. They'll say one thing but then do something completely different.

§ Values don't mean shit unless you *live* them. §

Don't just tell me what your values are; demonstrate them! Act on them. Especially if you're the founder. As a leader, you must deeply exemplify the company's virtues at all times and **live your culture in your own behavior.**

I'll give you an example. Early on in our company, at a monthly all-hands meeting, twenty-five to thirty of us were crammed into our shitty office overlooking a cemetery (seriously). I was talking to the group when the phone rang. Everyone just sat there and let it ring, including the folks from our customer service department. I was the CEO, and they didn't want to interrupt me. So I stopped the meeting, walked over to the customer service phone, and took the call myself. And I'm not even a native Portuguese speaker!

It was a teachable moment about being customer-obsessed: the virtue I wanted to convey to the team was that there's nothing more important than a customer. Little actions like that are real statements—and so important because they become lore. In a very real way, they become the *truth* in the company.

But only if you're taking genuine action. Action is everything. And with the initial set of virtues that Thomas and I came up with, they were all rooted in action. For example, when an intern spilled a beer in the office, I remember I got on my hands and knees before anyone else could and cleaned that shit up. Seems like a small thing, but it was a memorable action that demonstrated **humility**. This was one of our most important virtues—humility—and what made it so was that we put it into regular, daily practice.

To us, humility meant that you have to leave your ego at the door. It's not about the person; it's about the idea. *Best ideas win*, no matter where they come from. Or to put it another way, results are what count, and there are no fixed concepts or best practices, just best solutions. But again, all this emphasis on humility would have meant nothing if we hadn't demonstrated it in practice over and over again. Lots of companies talk about the spirit of serving other people. But if that's what you *say* you want, you have to back it up with really strong action.

More to the point, virtues aren't just about actions you intend to take but also past actions. For example, in starting our business and having trouble raising money, we went for a long time without a lot of cash. This taught us to **be frugal**. So when Thomas and I sought to explicitly carve out our virtues, we drew from our experiences up to that point—and being frugal was a big part of the journey we had lived through.

In those early days, when we were starting our Brazil operation, we also very much lived the virtue that we would come to describe as **make things happen**. Diego is a perfect example of this. I remember one time we had set up a meeting with the director of mortgage credit from Bradesco, and this fellow insisted on meeting us at *our* office, not theirs. But our "office," if you could call it that, was just part of the apartment building where Diego lived. We didn't even have a conference table. So the night before the meeting, we all drove to the furniture store and picked out a table. It was pouring rain outside when we tried to load it into Diego's car, only to discover that it wouldn't fit in the back of his little Fiat. So we had to put down the passenger seat, get the table in, and have me just lay flat on top of it for the entire ride. That was bad enough, but the table also encroached on Diego's manual transmission—so we had to drive all the way back only being able to shift between first, third, and fifth gear! Amazingly, we were able to get back to the apartment building in one piece and assemble the table in time for the meeting the next day. We *made it happen*. It was just the kind of people we were and had always been.

Sometimes, however, the virtues we arrived at came from the mistakes we made. In our early days, for example, we had struggled with our people being shy about speaking up and challenging us on important matters. Because of that, we learned just how important it is to actively foster an environment of questioning. Which led us to another virtue: **don't do anything you think is stupid**. In other words, if you are headed down the wrong path or making bad decisions, you need your team members to do what you're supposed to do on a New York City subway: see something, say something!

This virtue was actually based on a concept we got from Malcolm Gladwell's *Outliers*. In the book, he tells the story of a 1990 plane crash. Due to bad weather, the airplane had to circle JFK airport for over an hour until fuel levels were dangerously low. The pilot, who was Colombian, ordered the co-pilot, also Colombian, to tell air traffic control what was going on. New York air traffic controllers are known for being overly rude. And the co-pilot used a lot of mitigating speech patterns to downplay his opinions, which people tend to do when they want to sound polite or respectful before an authority. The co-pilot never asserted himself as much as he should have and never used the magic word "emergency." In the end, this turned out to be deadly—but the co-pilot wasn't the only one to blame. Flight attendants and a flight engineer had entered the cockpit and were aware of how serious the situation was, but no one said a thing. They were too worried they would seem too aggressive: the captain was the expert, and to question him would have been uncomfortable and potentially humiliating.

This was especially relevant for us at the time when we were building our company initially in Colombia. We didn't fully understand it yet, but there is something called the *¡Si, Señor* mentality that is especially prevalent in Colombia and Brazil. It means that you do whatever the boss says because they're the boss. This was the antithesis of what we wanted for our business. It went completely against our belief that what matters is not who comes up with the idea, but the idea itself.

Obviously, there are exceptions to this rule, and in the US startup scene, the pendulum almost swings too far in the opposite direction to the point that it becomes counterproductive. In the States, people love to challenge and get into debates about *everything*. But that was not the problem we had when we were launching our company. Our challenge was to get people past this harmful *¡Si, Señor* mentality. As the startup culture in Latin America grows, however, we see more people with the right fit for startup life. As the ecosystem develops, a new generation of people with an owner mentality is born.

We wanted to create a culture of being *bold*, and this spoke to another cultural virtue we defined at the beginning, which was to take risks, make mistakes, and learn from them. Don't sit on the sidelines, waiting for things to happen. Or, to put it another way, **it's better to ask for forgiveness than permission**. For example, in the early days, we had the chicken-and-egg problem with our marketplace, the question of what comes first, the property listing or the property searchers. In our case, we knew we needed to bring property inventory to our site. But nobody wanted to list their properties because we didn't have anyone searching! So we decided to build a bot that would search the web and scrape all the inventory from real estate brokers' websites.

It was a bold move and one that helped catapult us to growth. But immediately after going live with this strategy, we started to get tons of calls from potential customers threatening to sue us because we had never gotten their permission to include their properties. The only reason they found out about us was that they had started to receive a bunch of inbound contacts from our website—people looking to buy and rent the properties we scraped. Thankfully, we were quickly able to diffuse their anger by getting them to understand that we were actually generating value for them and weren't a threat to their business.

It was a big risk we took, but it paid off! We didn't ask for permission, and, in that case, we didn't even really ask for forgiveness. But eventually, after we converted those first few angry calls into trial customers, we did adapt our strategy and developed a more refined approach that wasn't perceived as so aggressive.

To be clear, these virtues—ask for forgiveness, not permission; don't do anything you think is stupid; etc.—weren't just ideas that Thomas and I came up with for the hell of it. After selecting these as our virtues, the whole point was to *communicate them* consistently and from the beginning with every new person who joined the company. No one was better at that than Diego. He'd literally sit people down and go through the whole set, reading each one aloud and explaining exactly why it was important.

Crucially, we did this right from the get-go, with the first people we hired. If you don't have a clear definition of what you believe in, right when you're starting out, your initial hires won't know what you stand for either. You've got to have your baseline DNA as a company, and that comes from the founders.

As you evolve as a company, certain virtues may take precedence over others. For example, in our early days, we were up against all odds. There was just so much shit we were dealing with. We needed our people to feel as supported as possible just to keep them fired-up through it all. So we made sure to celebrate their successes as much as possible, and in the beginning, **celebrating successes** was a no-brainer for our list of virtues. We knew we had to celebrate those small early wins to get our mojo going! It was almost like manifesting our future success.

But later on, this virtue wasn't quite as crucial. Yes, celebrating successes and appreciating the little wins is still relevant when you're a bigger company, but if you're not careful, it can backfire. Think about it: if you're winning and celebrating all the time, you run the risk of becoming arrogant. Next thing you know, you're unprepared when a smaller startup comes in and eats your lunch! I remember that this happened with our competitors: they were arrogant, and we took advantage of this vulnerability. But at other times, it was us on the wrong side of the equation: we were the arrogant ones struggling to adapt to the changing landscape.

It happens all the time: businesses are so busy celebrating their successes that they develop a blind spot. They wind up discounting their competitors to their own detriment. They're not on guard anymore, and that's exactly when the savvy newcomer decides to pounce.

When you start thinking you're the shit, you stop learning. Stay humble!

A lot of the virtues on our initial list spoke to this and tried to warn us against thinking we had all the answers. "Never settle, stay hungry," we wrote. And "Our customers have great ideas: listen." It was an interesting mix. On the one hand, we wanted to be conscious of any creeping arrogance, but we also needed to encourage the fighting spirit that is so important in a startup. One of our virtues, for example, was "Respect competitors but beat them in every way possible."

Then there were virtues that were more grounded in our day-to-day work, more product- and engineering-related. For example, our early experiences had taught us how to iterate fast when it came to cycles of product, and this led to a virtue that we described as "Release fast and release often."

Looking back now on that initial list that Thomas and I came up with, for the most part, I am impressed by how on-point the virtues were, even back then. There would be a number of iterations in the future, but the guiding principles remained the same.

HOW DO YOU COME UP WITH YOUR VIRTUES?

Back when I was only nineteen, I worked at a company, Z57. Then, I started a business of my own—not the real estate venture, this was even earlier—and tried to write out the virtues. Honestly, I just copied them from Z57. Literally, I went to their website and looked to see what *they* cared about.

Cool, I thought, *those sound like good ones, I'll use those.*

It's very hard to come up with your own virtues until you're actually *in it*, building the business. And even then, if you haven't already built a business before, you really don't know what you're doing. All you can do is study and pay close attention to what's going on around you in your new startup. Look at what it is that you and your co-founder or team are spending most of your energy on. Observe and reflect. Then, take those observations and reflections and come up with virtues around them.

In our case, Thomas and I drew from all the headaches we had suffered trying to build a business during the two years when it was just us. Then, we condensed all of that into something that felt meaningful and true to our experience.

Virtues can be as meaningful or meaningless as you choose to make them.

⸹ Make your virtues meaningful and authentic to you. ⸹

Your virtues are what will guide you and your people through the early years of your company. But at a certain point—for us, it was after the first 100 employees—you'll have to do a kind of reset where you ask yourself: **how do we now operationalize these virtues at scale?**

Renata Lorenz, who oversaw our HR, suggested we break our teams into small groups and ask them the question, "If you were starting a company on Mars, who would you bring and why?" The phrasing here was key: instead of asking them for descriptions of the virtues they cherished, we tried to get at the specific behavioral traits they admired in key people they worked with.

We did it this way because a lot of people have a hard time coming up with a set of virtues out of thin air; they're better at describing real-life actions that they've witnessed themselves.

For us founders, it was so insightful to hear about the behaviors that people valued inside our company (serves other people, etc.). The answers that emerged may not have differed radically from what we had first established on our own, but they created a *lot* more clarity.

From there, we put the behaviors into buckets and basically simmered them down like a reduction sauce to transform them into *virtues*. It was **a systemic way of integrating our virtues among a much bigger team.** Instead of just a random list, now we had a crystallized, streamlined version that we could condense down into even tighter subcomponents. It was all part of the process of operationalizing our virtues.

The Mars exercise also crucially helped build a deeper connection among our team because these virtues were created from the bottom up by the team members themselves.

But that didn't mean we could just rest on our laurels and expect the virtues to self-propagate on their own. We knew we had to constantly communicate these principles internally, day in and day out, to embed them through our organization. We did this through *stories*, dozens of them, told over and over to highlight behaviors.

CHALLENGES WITH COMMUNICATING YOUR VIRTUES

Obviously, as a founder, you have to have clarity on what you're trying to build and why. With Viva Real, this sense of purpose was clear to us in the early days of the company and well-communicated as part of our onboarding process when we brought on new people. We also made it a key element of our interviews with prospective hires.

But one of the challenges, especially for a venture-backed company, is how to maintain that attention to healthy communication as you scale your business.

When you're still at a certain size—say fifty to sixty people—it's easy as a founder to know everyone in the company. But when it gets beyond that, sometimes you start not knowing exactly who does what, or even not knowing everybody's name. (In the next chapter, we will talk about team size for early-stage startups and why you should keep your initial team small until you have built a product and received feedback and validation from the market.) If we hadn't have put in place a strong foundation for operationalizing our virtues and communicating them at scale, it would have been a complete disaster **when we went into hypergrowth-mode and suddenly found ourselves—within the span of one year—jumping in size from fifty to 250 people.** We were hiring twenty new employees each month!

Even as it stood, we suffered quite a bit during this time. Yes, we had invested in preparing to scale our culture, so we had some mechanisms to handle it. But in retrospect, we could have done a lot more and been better equipped.

When you read a document outlining a company's core values, you may retain a lot of it. But there's nothing like seeing real-life examples of these values personified and publicly recognized. People *really* remember those moments. But you also have to pay attention to how you frame the communications. If you really want to take advantage of the opportunity and use the occasion to drive home what you believe in as a company—so that it penetrates deep into the very fabric of your organization—your presentation and messaging is key.

In our case, whenever we took the opportunity to champion a certain virtue, we made sure to package it for maximum impact—by choosing the right time and place and the right words.

This is how you operationalize and scale your culture.

CHAPTER FIVE

EARLY-STAGE TEAMBUILDING AND DECISION-MAKING

There's a temptation in the early days of building a business to cut corners or make questionable decisions in order to jump-start your acceleration. But this is the most crucial time for founders to act in responsible, deliberate ways that will set the tone for the future—especially when it comes to hiring. Here, Brian reveals his own mistakes in being too lenient initially when it came to hiring for virtues. Although hustle is the number one requirement in an early startup, it's also true that someone who's a bad hire culturally will pollute the company like a virus from the inside out. Early-stage teambuilding at a startup is all about drawing people with the right profile—who are already philosophically and temperamentally inclined toward working for a startup—and weeding out those who aren't a fit. Brian would deliberately tell new hires, "This is going to be the hardest job you've ever had." Interviewing and hiring are of key importance, but they're far from the only challenging decisions founders will have to make when starting out. In the second half of the chapter, Brian walks readers

> through the early-stage processes of building an MVP, find-
> ing product-market fit, and validating the business. He and
> his co-founders had to make some enormously consequen-
> tial decisions themselves when they shifted their business to
> focus only on Brazil, which meant laying off a whole office
> in Colombia.

In the early days of Viva Real, we had a guy approach us about
potentially hiring him. He had worked for our competitor (at
the time, this other company was the Goliath to our David,
the successful incumbent we were trying to go up against) and
shockingly implied that if we hired him, he would bring us their
spreadsheet of customers. This is totally illegal, mind you, so
it was never really a hard decision on our part (even though
no one would have ever likely found out). But I bring it up
because **when you're struggling in the early days of building
your business, the temptation to cut corners and jumpstart
your acceleration is real**—particularly when you aren't funded
and are just trying to survive.

Thankfully, in the case of that particular fellow, we weren't
tempted. Not just because what he was proposing was illegal,
but also because it showed his character (or lack thereof). If
we had hired him and he brought this information, it could
have resulted in a quick burst of customers, but the culture
of the company would be eternally damaged. At some point,
he would have treated us the same way he was treating his
former employer.

To be totally honest, there *were* times when we hired questionable people. Not so much questionable ethically—and certainly
not on the level of doing anything illegal—but people who were
really good at their jobs but, deep down, we knew weren't the
right fit in terms of our virtues.

We were perhaps a little lenient in our early days when it came to the importance of *hiring for virtues*. It was understandable: at that stage in any business, you need people who can work their asses off and get the job done. But the problem with this line of thinking, of course, is that the early hires will, at some point, end up hiring other people!

If you bring on folks with the wrong set of virtues, you're laying bad groundwork for the future.

In the case of the guy who offered to bring us information from our competitor, again, it was pretty clear that someone like that would be a virus in the company, polluting it with the wrong DNA. But circumstances are not always so cut-and-dried. In the early days of building a business, founders are often confronted with very tough decisions. They have to weigh so many different factors, and often there are no great answers or solutions, only "less bad" ones.

As much as I wish I could say I would never make a decision that compromised the kind of company I was trying to build, it's not always so easy to take the high road—especially when you're running out of cash, figuring out how to make payroll, and so on.

My advice to founders: if you really have to get a certain job done to keep things moving and have no choice but to hire someone who is a questionable culture fit (maybe it's the only person you know who can do the task), just hire them as a temporary freelancer for the one thing and then move on with your business. It's not optimal, but sometimes it's a necessary compromise. It will allow you to keep moving forward while not taking a terrible toll on your culture in the long-term.

But don't make these decisions lightly. Learn from my mistakes. I know that with my next company, I will be ruthlessly focused on hiring for virtues from the beginning. I will make zero concessions.

The decisions you make in your early days as the founder of a startup are so important in how they set the tone for the future.

Nowhere is this more true than with hiring.

HOW TO THINK ABOUT HIRING IN EARLY-STAGE STARTUPS

First, how do you even know how many people you should try to hire in the early days of your company? What is the right team size?

Even if you have access to significant capital—and I will cover the topic of capital raising in-depth later in the book—the ideal team size initially is six to eight people. Why not more than that? When you're just starting out, you should be laser-focused on one thing, and that's finding **product-market fit (PMF)**. Product-market fit is the milestone where your customers perceive such great value in your product that they are willing to pay for and recommend it. And the ways you evaluate PMF are through such metrics as revenue, renewal rates, and Net Promoter Score (NPS).

Getting to PMF is a science and an art, but I firmly believe that a larger team makes it harder; too many cooks in the kitchen dramatically increases complexity and doesn't contribute proportionately to hitting this key milestone. With any team, it's a struggle to bring everyone along together so that you are all rowing in the same direction. The bigger the team, the more effort this takes, and founders often underestimate the cost. As Warren Buffett says, "You can't make a baby in one month by getting nine women pregnant."

You need a small and nimble team to get you to product-market fit, a core team that will go into battle with you. It is hard. It can be frustrating. And it is almost guaranteed that, when you finally launch your product after months of grinding away, you'll get negative feedback that makes you feel like crap. The smaller the team, the easier it is to battle through the early iterations. I can't stress this enough: it is so much easier to maintain the morale of a smaller group and rally them around what is mission-critical.

> Chaos is guaranteed. But if you hire properly, your tight-knit core team can rise up in the face of challenges.

There are certain people who thrive on solving hard problems. These are the people you need. During the early days of Viva Real, we had plenty of hard problems and the mantra inside our company was "adapt and overcome." I used to say it every day, all day.

Still, I made a lot of classic mistakes when we were starting out, like hiring a flashy executive from a larger company because he had so much impressive experience. There is simply no need for that when you're still in your early days as a business. It's no good for you *or* them. I also hired a director of marketing from a well-established company—and on his second or third day, he was already telling me, "Brian, here's the org chart I want." I had to set him straight: "Dude, it's just going to be you and one other person; you've got to be hands-on and get it done yourself." Of course, this disconnect could and should have been identified in the interviewing process, but when you are inexperienced at building a company, you make a lot of assumptions based on the candidate's previous work experience. Also, because you're just starting out, often you lack clarity around what you need.

In the early stage of building a business, it's a lot of just executing. Designing processes comes later. But you can still *prepare* to build those processes by taking the time to write stuff down. Any time you find yourself saying the same thing more than once or twice—giving the same advice or direction to your people—do yourself a favor and jot down your words. You definitely don't need to be heavy on process at this stage, but it's a great time to start thinking about how you can streamline.

Meanwhile, you need to find people who can hustle and execute. My rule of thumb in hiring is that hustle is *always* more important than brilliant intellect. But, in the beginning, this is especially true because without hustle, you won't survive to see another day.

One of my early employees liked to take his time and read the newspaper in the morning. He didn't last long. The image of him leisurely thumbing through his paper sent the wrong message to everyone else. Another early employee would leave right on the dot at 5 p.m. every day like a German train leaving the station. Look, there's nothing wrong with reading a newspaper or wanting to get back home to your family, but day after day, these behaviors came to symbolize a lack of hustle. I am not promoting a slave-to-the-company mentality but *read the paper at home*. Also, I always found it weird because our business was trying to kill the newspaper, so it made the message even worse!

Hustle and urgency are so important in those early days of a company when you need the high, fast-paced energy just to fight your way through.

> Hustle is the #1 requirement in the early days of a company.

What else should you be looking for?

WHAT TO LOOK FOR IN YOUR FIRST HIRES

How are you even supposed to know what you need, especially when it comes to hiring for roles you've never occupied or performed yourself? How can you know what you want if you've never done it before? How do you go about hiring a strong software engineer, for example, if you aren't an engineer?

It's not easy, but the answer is you have to get external guidance from respected people in the field, particularly when it comes to technical positions. Hopefully, you have people in your network that fit the bill. But if you don't, at the very least, you can give the candidate a quick project to test the water. Ask him or her to create a prototype for a certain feature and give them only one day to perform the task. Even though you aren't an engineer, you should be able to tell a lot from the speed and quality with which the person approaches the project.

That said, if at all possible, you should get outside advice. The consequences of a bad hire are just too great and ignorance is not an excuse. **If you don't know what you want, you won't know if you've found the right person.** You have to be clear on what strengths you're looking for in the person and also what forms of weakness you are okay with. The reality is you're probably not going to find (or have the resources to hire) the *perfect* person, especially in the beginning. So you have to define what's acceptable to you in terms of skill gaps.

For example, if you're hiring someone to lead the engineering team, is it more important for that person to have really strong technical chops or people management skills? If it's the latter, and you're looking for them to help scale your team, maybe it's okay that they don't have the latest tech stack knowledge, that they're a few years behind the curve. Maybe what's more important to you is that they've been working in the field a long time, and have experience managing engineering teams—in which case you would probably be willing to tolerate their lack of current tech knowledge (and instead bring in someone else to help in that department).

Again, clarity is everything when it comes to hiring, and the best way to gain clarity on what you want if you're *not* well-versed yourself is to talk to people who are. But founders are sometimes insecure about this and think they have an expert understanding themselves when they really don't.

> If you're not knowledgeable about what it is you're hiring for, you have to accept and come to grips with that—or you're going to a mistake that could cost you dearly down the road.

Sure, you can learn a lot from interviews, but that is not a good mechanism for educating yourself. If you're using the interview process as your main source of information, you're going to wind up relying too heavily on that one piece of the hiring puzzle. You're going to make bad decisions based on a vague feeling: who *feels good* to you in the context of an interview. You may even become susceptible to bias, to hiring based on how someone looks or talks. I made this mistake early on, as I was admittedly biased to prospects who spoke better English. But the reality was that this language skill wasn't even that important for most roles. So why was I putting so much value on it?

Another area worth flagging is what I would call the confidence gap. Men are often overconfident in interviews compared to women. Their skills may be at the same level, but men tend to *think* they are more capable than they actually are. I have seen this a lot in the hiring process. But back in our early days, I actually didn't do a lot of the interviews myself because I didn't speak very good Portuguese yet. Diego was extremely helpful when it came to interviewing—and teambuilding in general.

But because we didn't have an office in those days, he'd have to do the interviews at the local Starbucks. It made us both a little self-conscious. In retrospect, having to do interviews at the coffee shop was great because it showed prospective hires *who we really were*—and **weeded out anyone who wasn't already philosophically and temperamentally inclined toward working for a scrappy startup like ours.**

Diego interviewed our very first hire, Vanessa, in that Starbucks. At the time, she was working at MercadoLibre. So the fact that she wasn't turned off by the humble digs (or lack of digs whatsoever) showed us she was down for the cause and definitely the right person for the job. Even though she already had a stable gig, she was more excited about what we were doing—and ready to jump on board.

On our part, again, it helped that we weren't pretending to be something we weren't—or sugarcoating how hard it was going to be. In fact, I encourage founders to set the expectation in those first interviews that it's going to be a rough journey ahead. I always used to tell people in the interview: "This is going to be the hardest job you've ever had." It might have been a slight exaggeration, but better to open that way than to tell them, "Oh, this is going to be so much fun, you're going to be amazing," and then at the first sign of difficulty, have them realize with a shock that it's not what they signed up for.

You want to scare them just a little bit. Okay, not *scare* them, but create an expectation that the job is going to be something challenging and way different than what they're used to.

The fact that Vanessa welcomed this challenge said a great deal about her. It also probably spoke to our contagious co-founder energy in those early days. What do I mean by co-founder energy? It's a real thing, a superpower. As co-founder, you are so passionate about what you are doing that your excitement infects everyone you talk to. It's also why people are so attracted to projects that are purpose-driven.

With Vanessa and others, we came to realize that **natural selection tended to draw the right profile in the people we hired**, and so we leaned into it. Instead of trying to hide all the aspects of the business that could be perceived as disadvantages, we came right out with them. We were completely transparent that this thing we were working on didn't have much form yet, we didn't have an office or even a conference table, and the new hires would be making their own coffee.

The beauty of putting all our unappealing cards on the table like that was that it had the effect of self-selecting men and women with the right DNA, who were excited about the challenge of building something from nothing.

You can pretty much tell if a person you're considering hiring is all the way in, ready to jump in the trenches with you, or if they're hesitant. But that doesn't mean you won't have to put on the hard sell sometimes if you're trying to recruit someone. To be clear, you shouldn't ever play it cool. You *should* let the person know how much you want them. When you're hiring your first executives, don't treat it like dating. Don't dance around the issue ("Hey, we're kind of interested."). Be straightforward. Be aggressive.

I know that whenever I was trying to recruit someone, I would do whatever it took: meet with spouses and parents, take prospects out to dinner, go on jogs and bike rides with them, even cook for them (and I'm a pretty bad cook). You need to go the extra mile and proclaim your love.

But that doesn't mean sugarcoating how hard it's going to be or what the scrappy startup life is really like. If the person is asking you questions in the interview about bonuses, that's a red flag that they're not the right fit—not cut out for the inherent risk involved. Or they're just inexperienced and have no idea how startups work, which is why they're asking all the same silly job interview questions that they've been taught to their whole lives. In either case, I would politely explain to them that the physics of an early-stage startup is different—the company likely isn't even making money at this point—and see how they react.

> You can't have bonuses in a company in the beginning—especially if your company is still losing money.

Interviewing and hiring in the early days of a business can definitely be eye-opening. Early-stage teambuilding in general is a huge learning experience. It was for me.

But let there be no confusion: these are far from the only challenging, consequential decisions you'll have to make when you're starting out.

If your journey is like mine, you may also have to make decisions that result in painful layoffs.

EARLY-STAGE DECISION-MAKING

As readers know by now, initially, we were based in Colombia. We had markets there, Mexico, and Brazil—but all the business was handled out of our headquarters (if you can call it that) in Colombia. Later, we realized that the market in Brazil was just massively larger and riper with opportunity than the others. In fact, there were more potential customers in the state of Rio de Janeiro alone than in the entire country of Colombia.

When it came to product-market fit, our problem was a little different: although we had *product fit* and could see that we were generating value with our business out of Colombia, we knew we were in the *wrong* market.

So we decided to go **AAB: All About Brazil**.

It was the right decision, but it meant we had to fire a bunch of people in our Colombia office. We had twenty team members there and ended up making offers to some of them to move to Brazil. Four accepted. I remember being really worried about what would happen to the others. It was absolutely the right business decision; if we hadn't made the move, the business would have likely failed. But that didn't make it any less miserable for the people we had to let go.

I could never have predicted what happened next: my fears about the fate of my former team members turned out to be almost completely unfounded. Carlos ended up running small-to-medium businesses (SMBs) for Facebook in Sao Paulo. Another got a really good government job making way more money than he ever did with me. Another woman went to MercadoLibre. In short, everyone did fine. Better than fine.

What I hadn't fully realized is that the environment we'd built had accelerated *all* of our growth. When you're working in a startup, you progress a lot faster because you're given so much more responsibility.

Also, because the emerging tech ecosystems in places like Colombia were growing at such a rate, it was a real asset in the job market to have worked at a tech company like ours. As for our former employees, it turned out that their perceived personal value, their individual stock as a professional, had shot up as a result of having worked in such an environment.

> Building a business from the ground up is an amazing way to accelerate personal and professional growth—not just for the founder but the whole team.

Having to make such a big shift so early on with our business— in terms of geographical focus but also with the layoffs—was an incredibly valuable lesson and one that's relevant to anyone just starting out in building their company. What I learned, above all, was **don't bother to build a big ol' business plan**. There's no point. It will grow old as soon as the ink dries. Everything you've strategized for so long, all your well thought out tactics can go out the window in an instant when a new and better opportunity or direction becomes apparent. That's a good thing. But it means you have to be ready to change course at any moment.

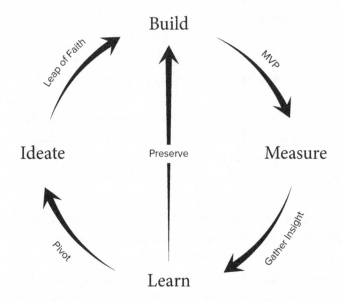

In our case, we saw the opportunity in Brazil, so we upped and moved our business there. It took courage, and it meant sacrificing a lot of what we had built so far—but it was absolutely the right move.

When it comes to early-stage decision-making, it's all about assessing the level of risk and finding the sweet spot. You don't want to jump blindly off a cliff, but sometimes you do want to sacrifice comfort and stability in the short-term like we did in moving our business to Brazil for a greater and more enduring opportunity.

Making big decisions like this for your business is so important, but it's exactly what we're taught *not* to do at most companies. You always have to remember that startups are different.

Whereas large established companies are trying to preserve their existing revenue, startups are hungrily looking for revenue. And the way they do that is by making bold decisions that change everything.

In fact, many successful startups have had at least one major pivot over the course of its history. YouTube, for example, started as an online dating site. Groupon started as a site for collective action.

In almost every case, you'll find that the decision to pivot was based on assessing market risk versus execution risk and ultimately *building something people want*. It's the same kind of thinking that goes into choosing an idea in the first place. Often, founders want to play it safe, and there's the temptation to just clone existing products. That's a mistake. "On the other hand," says five-time founder, product designer, and investor James Currier, "100 percent original product ideas are unlikely to work. The sweet spot is what I call 'new energy.'"

Whether you're trying to find the right balance between the originality of your product idea and the market risk involved or between sticking to your business plan versus dramatically changing course, one thing's for sure: your journey to get to the other side of the issue you're grappling with is going to be bumpy—but worth it in the end, if you do it right.

GROWING PAINS IN EARLY-STAGE PROCESSES

All in all, I believe it's good to have to struggle in the early days of building a business—because of what you learn from the experience. I see this even now as an investor. With companies whose success has come easy from the start, they don't look for the best answers in the same way. They also just throw money at problems because they have a lot of it. (The exception here is the veteran entrepreneurs who have done it before. Mistakes and experience are the greatest teachers.)

I tend to fall more on the "lean startup" way of thinking, which I will describe further in the coming pages. Especially nowadays, when I'm investing in companies, again, I'm drawn to those that have had to scrape by and hustle because I think it creates the right DNA in a business. But when a company is just handed a bunch of money, they're not pushed and challenged in the same way.

Then again, it's also important for early-stage businesses to not let themselves be limited in scope or vision because they can't see past their immediate struggles. Frankly, I think we fell victim to this tendency with some of the decisions we made. Because we didn't have much money, we weren't able to really see our future in the way founders ideally should—as a series of sequential breakthroughs to pursue. This probably led to our having a delayed response to competitors. We were just so worried about getting through the problems at hand, in the present moment, that we held ourselves back in certain ways.

This is also one of the reasons that experienced entrepreneurs, in contrast to novices, are often equipped to handle more capital. They've developed a kind of pattern recognition that allows them to look into the future and see clearly both the problems *and* opportunities. But many first-time entrepreneurs don't have this ability—and if you get a ton of money from investors, it can be pretty risky.

As for how to run your business financially in the early stages, I tend toward the lean startup model. If you want to learn more about this, there are entire books, YouTube videos, and podcasts about it. But basically, it's a methodology that allows you to fail and learn quickly, rather than waste lots of money. You never know when capital and access to funding is going to dry up. These things happen in cycles, and there are always unexpected events like we saw with the coronavirus pandemic of 2020. When money is flowing, the risk is that you end up thinking you can go faster in building your business than you actually can.

The lean startup model will help you steer clear of this pitfall. As you go through your early-stage processes of building an MVP, finding product-market fit, and validating your business, this approach will streamline your efforts and help minimize the time you waste on the thing you're building. The way it works is you do a series of *micro-experiments* that allow you to validate ideas quickly by gathering data and talking to customers.

Because you are bootstrapping it like we were, you're more resourceful. You set the goals and hypotheses of your experiment, then plan and prepare the tools you need to conduct it. After you run the experiment, you write down the numbers and results, then analyze them and draw conclusions. That's really what you're doing *all day long* in the early stages of your startup. The conclusions you make from the data are what push you in new directions and inspire you to take bold action. But as we'll see in the following chapter, sometimes it's not about deciding what to do but rather what *not* to do.

CHAPTER SIX

DECIDING WHAT *NOT* TO DO

Founders have to be very careful with the decisions they make. But deciding what not to do can be as important as deciding what to do. Entrepreneurs love to chase the bright and shiny lights, but if their attention is spread in a hundred different directions, they may miss their golden goose. From his advisor and investor, Simon Baker, Brian learned a lesson about the value of simplicity—"vanilla, vanilla, vanilla"—and why less is more. He calls upon readers to always be obsessing over activities that will generate the biggest impact and minimize waste with low-impact activities. He also shows how to mobilize your teams around these high-impact areas of focus.

I once asked a prominent founder, "What was the most important thing you did as you scaled your business?" I wanted to pick his brain for the biggest, best piece of advice. What he told me took me by surprise. He said I should physically write down all the things I know I'm *not* going to do in my business. Then, I should tuck away that list in a locked drawer as a symbolic way of saying, "I'm closing this door, I'm shutting off these avenues."

I get where he was going with that. As Steve Jobs famously said, deciding what *not* to do—especially as you move past the scrappy, early days of your company and into the growth stage—is as important as deciding what to do.

Every successful company has its golden goose. **If your attention is spread in a hundred different directions, you may miss your golden goose.** Entrepreneurs love to chase the bright and shiny lights. But in order to be successful and really gain the traction you need, you've *got* to cut out the distractions and drill down on what's essential. Bill Gates says you should focus 80 percent of your attention on 80 percent of your revenue. This is why founders have to actually look closely at their numbers to find the most important part of their business. If you mess this up, if you try to tackle a bunch of different ideas or initiatives—while likely not doing *any* of them as well as you could—you and your business may not survive at all.

⸝ Entrepreneurs love to chase the bright and shiny lights. ⸝

I definitely learned the importance of deciding what *not* to do when we made the call to exit those other countries and focus only on the Brazilian market.

But even before that, we learned a similar lesson when we came to recognize the value in the *simplicity* of our product, in contrast to our competitors who were using very complex pricing tiers. It was our investor Simon Baker who helped me see the light. Up to that point, we were trying to gain an edge by building a model that was cheaper than the incumbents. The competition was offering listing packages of twenty, fifty, one hundred, five hundred, or a thousand properties, and there was a tiered pricing system based on which option they chose. This model is what existed in the market, and we were the same but just offered lower prices. Not a very winning strategy.

After six months of trying to compete based on price, I had a conversation with Simon that changed everything. "**Vanilla, vanilla, vanilla,**" he said. What on earth did that mean? He advised us to radically simplify our model so that we only had one product. With this new approach, the real estate companies would list *all* their properties, and there would only be one price. No longer would they have to make a choice about the number of properties and pricing. It took all the complexity out of the sales process.

Now, there was no vanilla or chocolate or strawberry. It was just vanilla.

After making this change, almost immediately we saw an increase in the volume of sales per salesperson. With only one product to sell, our people could now be that much more efficient. Meanwhile, the consumers—the folks looking for an apartment—got a better experience because there was more inventory, which, in turn, drove more value to the marketplace.

It was what we call a "virtuous cycle."

So simple and so effective.

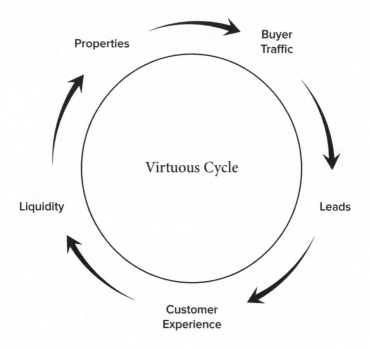

Properties

Buyer Traffic

Virtuous Cycle

Liquidity

Leads

Customer Experience

LESS IS MORE

When you're simplifying, or deciding what not to do, it's really all about calibrating effort versus impact.

As you can see in the graph below, your sweet spot—in terms of your direction at any given moment in a business—lies at the nexus of high-impact and low-effort. Activities that fall into that quadrant of the graph are precisely the ones you want to prioritize. Clearly, the opposite is also true: you should **steer clear of activities with low-impact that require high-effort.** You'll just be swimming against the tide, for little payoff.

It's almost a cliché now, but you always want to be *obsessing* over the activities that will generate the biggest impact—and conversely, you want to minimize waste, i.e., the amount of time, energy, and resources, you put into low-impact activities.

But it's also important to recognize the value in activities that are, for example, high-impact and high-effort, where the impact is so profound that it's worth putting in all that effort. In fact, this is often where the biggest opportunities lie, as many companies don't want to do the hard work and instead stick to low-hanging fruit. As my friend and co-founder at Latitud Yuri Danilchenko says, "If you want to make a Tesla, you better roll up your sleeves for some hard work."

To be clear, this doesn't mean you have to do something no one has ever done before. To paraphrase Alex Atala, one of the world's best chefs: the secret is not to prepare a dish that nobody else ever has, but rather to make a familiar dish and do it better. This is a good reminder that founders don't need to be so obsessed with innovation. Unlike in the academic world, where you have to invent something new or else your paper won't be published, with startups, you just have to make the product work—*either* by inventing something new or making something that already exists better.

Many markets are still underserved, but it's not because of a lack of innovative ideas. It's because the existing companies didn't deliver on their promises, don't actually have a customer-centric mentality, or are missing some essential part of the complete product that the customer needs to solve his or her pain.

So, *do* pay attention to high-impact, high-effort activities when warranted, but *don't* obsess over having to build something entirely new.

Also, make sure you don't ignore the low-effort, low-impact activities. Why *not* attack the low-hanging fruit if it's right there and it's so easy?

Just don't let it distract you from your main area of concentration. That's really what this is all about. There's a tendency among founders and entrepreneurs to spread themselves too thin—and then they end up wondering why they haven't achieved the results they were after! It's because they made the mistake of getting in their own way.

If only they could understand and accept the simple truth that **sometimes less is more.**

> There are so many different things you can do, but when you find something really significant that generates a lot of impact, you should laser in and obsess over it.

In the startup world, there's also a common misconception that when you have more resources, you can and should do more. Companies go on hiring sprees, bringing on tons of people to attack problems in every direction. The truth is there's no equation that says if you double the size of your team, it will double the output.

No matter how much money you have, you should always be thinking about how you design your teams and always focus your energy on what really matters: building a good, profitable business that grows and impacts your customer.

There's no one-size-fits-all advice here. It's about identifying the area or areas in *your* business that will generate the most value—no matter your level of resources.

When you're flush with cash, again, it's easy to fall into the trap of believing you can do everything. You wind up wasting time on nonsense. In our case, honestly it probably helped that we didn't have much money. I'm sure we still did stuff that wasn't important (like going overboard with the design of our logo, which didn't really make a difference to our customer experience), but in general, having to basically bootstrap our business made it that much easier to prioritize. We didn't have a choice.

Even though we had long-term priorities such as the architecture of our site, customer service, partnerships, benchmarking, PR, and of course, sales, in the short-term, sometimes other items took precedence. For example, there was a period where we just decided to put all big goals on the back burner and obsess over *two things and two things only*: listings (i.e., properties) and traffic (specifically Search Engine Optimization or SEO for Google). We gave ourselves an intentional case of tunnel-vision and didn't even talk about anything else.

It may sound extreme, but when you consciously put on those blinders and zero in with fierce determination on something very specific, wow, it just unleashes so much value.

Along the same lines, as CEO, I used to have an initiative called Theme of the Year. We had Year of the Consumer, Year of 5,000 Customers, Year of Integration, and more. This framing helped us get over our struggles with quarterly planning and created a laser-beam focus among our team, which is *so* important: after all, **you can do a great job as founder to identify the high-impact activities and areas of focus, but it means nothing if you can't mobilize your team around those choices.**

Of course, you don't want your theme or focus to lock you in when your business is evolving. And the Theme of the Year approach will only work if you already have a lot of clarity in your business and have nailed (but not scaled) it already. You have to stay flexible as you grow—still obsessed with your idea and whatever aspect of it is poised to generate the highest impact, but with the clarity to pivot or iterate if it's not working or if the needs of your company change.

I was just okay at this. I didn't evolve the business as much as I could have. In particular, we were ineffective ultimately at adapting to new entrants who out-innovated us. In the early days of building Viva Real, *we* were the disruptors. The incumbents—there were several existing players—were slow, entrenched in their ways, and couldn't adapt to the changes we brought to the market. We built a lot of value, but then we made some of the same mistakes ourselves. For example, we should have launched our own version of Quinto Andar in partnership with our customers. QA hadn't started out as a competitor, but if I had possessed more humility at that point, I would have seen them coming. We left the door open for them and also for Loft, a new startup that has now raised hundreds of millions of dollars.

We did plenty wrong, but we also did a lot right. And I credit the Theme of The Year for helping us focus. Obviously, it didn't mean we forgot about everything else for the next 365 days. But it gave us a hugely useful frame to guide and help us understand what we were all about. Then, at the end of the year, we would always reflect on what we got right and wrong.

NAIL IT BEFORE YOU SCALE IT

In retrospect, what we did really well as we grew was bring on some very strong people who got into execution-mode and were just superstars operationally. They understood through and through the importance of *nail it before you scale it*—and once we nailed it, they were incredibly good at scaling it.

Whereas in the early days we were just kind of fumbling around, looking for product-market fit, now the name of the game was to be as surgical and measured as possible. You iterate, you test, and see what works. On the one side, you have your repeatable process or business opportunity. On the other, you have your team (your existing people or new folks you bring on). "Nail it before you scale it" means bringing those two things together: the team takes the repeatable opportunity and scales it to the next level so that you're able to deliver like never before on the process and execute your growth plan.

It was 2010 when we found product-market fit. That was before the whole lean startup movement. I wish I had read that book— *The Lean Startup* by Eric Ries—before we spent those years fumbling around trying to figure out exactly where we were. But we did have the advantage of being inspired by other similar businesses around the world. Seeing what they did shortened the learning curve and allowed us to avoid wasting too much time on stuff that had already been proven not to work.

Going out and speaking to all these people who had done it before in other markets was a real turning point for me and our business. It helped us craft a clear roadmap on how to execute—and it just goes to show how important it is to have investors, mentors, and advisors like this who you can lean on.

In the following chapter, we look at the role of boards and advisors.

CHAPTER SEVEN

MY ADVICE ABOUT ADVISORS AND BOARDS

A good advisor can validate your thinking, and that alone is a massive accelerator. Fear of the unknown has led many a founder into a dreaded state of overanalyzing, but an advisor can help break this impasse. Typically, advisors are given shares in the company in exchange for their participation, but Brian believes it's better to have them put in their own money—so they have some skin in the game. His own early advisors were his dad (an entrepreneur himself) as well as his good friend, who had already achieved a successful exit. From there, Brian wanted to bring on "smart money" with his fundraising, i.e., experienced investors who could help guide and support him. Startup boards can be incredibly valuable—in helping to recruit talent and make introductions, as well as lending credibility to your business—but they can also be highly ineffective. There's no need for an early-stage company to have a formal board: you'll wind up using it as just a reporting mechanism, which is a big waste of time. When you do start assembling your board members, however, you want to focus on people who have built successful businesses before, experienced entrepreneurs or investors who have the right attitude and are committed to playing an active role. Finally, don't make the mistake that Brian did of using board meetings to sell your investors on the business. They're already invested!

When Thomas and I were just starting out and struggling to raise capital to get off the ground, we had a real breakthrough moment when we found Simon Baker, an incredible advisor with tons of experience operating and executing the same type of business as ours in Australia. Here was someone who had *been there* and understood, through and through, the challenges we were going to face as our company grew.

It's not that I just blindly followed everything he said, but I did really listen and internalize his key points. Often, I found that I already knew the right answer, but having him confirm my instincts meant everything.

I want to be very clear about this: you shouldn't expect (or even want) your advisors to *tell* you how to run your business. If you have an advisor making a bunch of decisions *for you*, something's off. You are not in the right place. However, an advisor can and should listen to you and give you perspective. They can play a similar role, in a way, to a therapist. Again, most of the time, deep down, you will know the right decision—but an advisor can give you the confidence to act on it.

It helps a lot. In your early days as a founder, you constantly doubt yourself, wondering whether you're on the right path. **Having a good advisor to validate your thinking is, in itself, a massive accelerator.** In a world where speed is a superpower, anything that can get you where you want to go faster is a huge boon to your success.

Simon was definitely that for us. I remember one time in particular when I was freaked out by a threat from a competitor, stuck in a state of overanalyzing, and Simon was there to talk me off the ledge. This competitor had just made a big acquisition: a software company, the same software company that *we* were using to supply us with data. My fear was that this source of data would be cut off from us.

I called Simon and he immediately calmed me down. He then asked if he could go back to sleep. He was in Australia, and I had called him in the middle of the night. I had been totally overthinking it. He explained why I didn't have to worry and why my fears were unfounded. He assured me the competitor wouldn't cut off our line to the data we needed—and he was absolutely right.

The details of the incident aren't even important. What matters is that he saved me from getting all twisted up in my head and paranoid about a threat that was nonexistent. It's a great example of how an advisor can protect you from unnecessary headaches—and put up those crucial guardrails, so you don't mentally unravel.

Simon was also the one who helped us make the important decision not to expand to other countries but instead do the exact opposite and focus only on Brazil. We had other investors at the time who thought differently: they advocated a regional approach where we would expand into more countries.

I am forever grateful we listened to Simon. If we had followed the path of focusing on many different markets, we would have likely been number three, trailing way behind the market leader everywhere we went. There would have been very little opportunity for value creation.

You've got to *win* a market. If you're not number one, the value goes way down. And if you're not number two, forget about it. In an industry like ours, in a mature market, the margins for the market leader should be around 50 percent—compared to 20 percent for the number two. At number three, you have virtually no margin at all.

The AAB (All About Brazil) strategy that we landed on seems so obvious now. I am not suggesting that a company should never expand regionally or internationally, but there is a huge advantage to winning the biggest market first. It's a question of going wide versus deep. We chose the latter, and when you go deep, you create more "moats" between you and your competitors. Your revenue is more defensible because you are the market leader.

Simply put, it's better to be number one in the biggest market than number two or three in a bunch of disparate markets. In fact, many high-growth startups in Latin America are now dividing their markets into even more localized units, i.e., focusing on cities, not countries—going deep with individual metropolises rather than trying to cover lots of broad markets. As for us, the decision to go AAB was something we went back and forth on for many months. Ultimately, we decided that the value of Brazil—and the opportunity cost of thinking about any other markets that weren't Brazil—might put at risk our desire for clear leadership, which we knew would eventually translate to higher margins.

But the decision could have gone either way. We had other smart, educated investors who disagreed with Simon's stance. Simon had a pretty strong perspective on this. He was the former

CEO of the market leader in the same business in Australia. He also runs events that bring together C-Level executives to talk about trends in this space. Simon knew that there was not one existing global online real estate company that had successfully expanded to other countries, and it was his very specific sector understanding that won out in the end.

SHOULD YOU GIVE EQUITY TO YOUR ADVISORS?

When you have an advisor, it's generally understood that you're giving them shares in the company, usually in the form of common stock, in exchange for their participation. This is how it's typically done, but I think it's a mistake. Better to have advisors put in their own money. It can be a relatively small sum—$10,000, $15,000, $25,000—but symbolically, they have skin in the game.

For better or worse, **an advisor thinks of their role differently when they've put in their own money, and not just been given equity**. Even now, as an investor, when someone asks me to be an advisor and offers me equity, I turn it down. I have to practice what I preach. And back when I was first starting out with Viva Real, most of the advisors I brought on put money in themselves. The few early advisors who didn't have skin in the game rarely stepped up. I'm not saying it can't work, but I think there's a strong psychological commitment in coming out of pocket, and it creates a feeling of being in the foxhole with the founder. When they invest, you can also top them off with additional equity for their involvement.

§ Advisors should be investors.   §

When you're trying to get off the ground, your first tier of investors is usually what's known, fondly, as FFF: Family, Friends, and Fools. This is what I did too, and there's nothing wrong with it. You'll remember I took money from my dad and also my good friend. (Neither of them are anybody's fools, by the way!). But then, after that, my fundraising became coupled with the process of bringing on more sophisticated investors. I didn't just want regular money; I wanted smart money, i.e., experienced investors who could help guide and support me toward generating tremendous impact.

It's worth mentioning that on the far opposite end of the spectrum from smart money, there's also what you would call "harmful money." That's when someone puts money in and mistakenly thinks they know what's best and ends up leading you in a terrible direction. This typically comes in the form of an investor who wants to buy a significant, sometimes controlling stake in a startup—and is usually the kiss of death for a startup that wants to be venture-backed. (We will talk more about the "cap table" and venture terms in Part Three.)

Thankfully, I was able to steer clear of those. Instead, I brought on a number of incredible individuals who would eventually make up our valuable board of advisors.

HOW SHOULD YOU THINK ABOUT DEVELOPING YOUR BOARD OF ADVISORS?

First things first: you need to understand the difference between a board of advisors and a board of directors (board members). A board of advisors is usually made up of industry experts who act independently. They don't even need to formally get together, but they are accessible to the CEO.

In my case, I personally leaned on the following individuals: Micky Malka, Kevin Efrusy, Simon Baker, Pete Flint, Greg Waldorf, and Shaun Di Gregorio, among others. These are all people who put money into the business and also came with general guidance and feedback. Even if we didn't all meet in the same room, I could call each of them and ask about specific situations.

A board of directors, on the other hand, is a formal reporting entity that is responsible for hiring and firing the CEO and supporting the company.

If you're an early-stage company, you don't need a formal board of directors. It's a waste of time.

For early-stage companies who haven't yet raised institutional capital, there's really no point in having a board. Founders wind up using it as nothing more than a reporting mechanism—and it's meaningless to report back to your board every month when your business is still in its infancy. What are you even going to have to talk about? You've got so much going on already when you're trying to get your business off the ground. Preparing a nonsense presentation every month is unnecessary. If you need to report something back to your investors, just do it independently on an informal basis.

When you do set up a more formal board, send around all the data beforehand. Don't use valuable meeting time to present the numbers. If the investors have any questions about the information you've sent, you can talk about it *then*. But if you go into a board meeting and present a deck in that setting, without them first knowing what to expect, you will waste time.

If you expect that there will be sensitive discussions, you should have individual calls with board members before the meeting to get aligned in advance. Otherwise, when you get in that room, it will just become a ping-pong match of people lobbying their opinions.

> Boards are a waste of time for early-stage companies. You'll just be using it as a reporting mechanism, and boards aren't (or at least shouldn't be!) designed for just reporting.

Board meetings *are* eventually going to become important. Don't set a crappy tone at the beginning. You want to orient your board to be *productive*—and if you're just using it as a formal reporting system, you're establishing a bad precedent.

Ultimately you're going to *need* a great, high-functioning board. You will draw from the accumulated experience and expertise of these board members. You will use them to help recruit talent and make introductions. They will also lend credibility to your business, especially if they've been part of a very successful project themselves.

So, how can you go about putting together the kind of board that is going to best serve you in all of these areas?

From what I've seen, the most effective, productive boards are the ones where there's a real connection and trust between the founder or CEO and his or her board members and board of advisors. Beyond that, the most important factor, in my experience, is to have people in both entities *who have built businesses before.*

Sometimes, this doesn't apply because the board members are investors, not entrepreneurs themselves—but they have a lot of experience serving on boards.

The point is: you want people who *know* how to do this, how to make the most out of boards and board meetings.

EFFECTIVE AND INEFFECTIVE BOARDS

I've seen plenty of meetings where board members are on their phones for the duration of the meeting, not participating at all. They're hardly even observing! Now, in some cases, a board member is literally just a *board observer*—technically, they're a member, but they don't have a vote. That's not what I'm talking about here. Rather, I'm referring to advisors who just don't take their responsibilities seriously. They're busy thinking about their own businesses and their own deals and not paying attention whatsoever. It's crazy: **why have a bunch of people sitting around a table doing nothing?**

Even if they're not on their phones, even if they're vocal, all too often, it feels like a performance, with people trying to sound smart but not actually adding value. I've seen this myself on various boards, but I've also heard it from a lot of other entrepreneurs.

Startup boards can be incredibly valuable, or they can be basically useless. The good news is that, as founder, you can play a big part in making your board an important vehicle for growth. But only if you use it in the right way.

When I was starting out, for example, I misunderstood the purpose of board meetings. I was still in the mindset of trying to sell investors on the business. So I spent our first couple of meetings reinforcing how great our company was. What I didn't realize was that, duh, these folks were already invested. I didn't have to persuade them anymore. They were on board (literally and figuratively!) and *wanted* me to do well.

> You don't have to use your board meetings to further sell
> yourself or prove your worth—your investors are already
> stockholders.

I'm not alone in making the mistake of using board meetings to
resell investors on the business. It's very common among early-
stage, venture-backed companies (Series A). This approach
might make sense *after* you've raised institutional capital. But
until that point, it's a waste of everyone's time to just talk about
everything that's going well.

Yes, you want everyone to be excited about the business; you
don't want them to lose confidence. But in that case, what you
should be doing at your board meetings instead is defining or
identifying your areas of focus. You should be talking about
how different aspects of the business are going. In the early
days, I used a red/yellow/green model where we'd take ten main
concepts and score ourselves. Obviously, green meant we were
doing well, yellow meant just okay, and red meant *watch out*.
We used that methodology for many years and repeated the
exercise every quarter to measure our progress. It was helpful
because it opened up the conversation where we could give
more context to the investors. No matter what, your investors
will never have even a fraction of the understanding of the
business that you have.

Over those years, we also came to see the power in **engaging our
management team to present at board meetings**. We didn't do
this at first, but once we made the change, our executives felt so
much more connected to the company. Exposing them to the
investors made them feel important—and they *were*.

Once you have a fully-baked executive team, you should definitely get them involved with your board. You shouldn't be running everything yourself. As CEO or founder, you need to always be teeing up your executives, helping them grow more comfortable communicating with your board. Your team has so much knowledge to share as your business grows. Your job is to facilitate their communicating that knowledge to your board.

Of course, that doesn't mean you should let your board meetings get bogged down with endless updates from each executive. Again, the purpose of these meetings is not for everyone to report back on what they've been doing. But if you're not careful, this is exactly what will happen. I suggest "timeboxing"—setting in advance a fixed, maximum amount of time for the meeting and sticking to it. In fact, I recommend designating someone specifically to hold the management team accountable for not going off on lengthy tangents.

Trust me; these board meeting discussions can go down a rabbit hole if you let them. As CEO, you've *got* to direct people and reel them back in.

Of course, your board members have some responsibility here too. You should be clear in what you're asking and expecting of them. First, they should come to the meeting having already read all the material. If they haven't done so, you should call them out for it. Yes, you're working for the board in that ultimately you report to them, and they have the ability to hire and fire the CEO. But the reality—at least with good, high-functioning boards—is that the board members are serving the team too.

Therefore, to serve the team well, the board members must be up on the materials so they're not wasting everyone's time trying to frantically read while in the meeting.

Apart from what they bring to the table as experienced entrepreneurs or investors, do the people you're asking to join your
board have the right *attitude* for it?

WHO DO YOU WANT ON YOUR BOARD?

You need to find board members with a certain level of matu-
rity. You want people who are genuinely supportive and who
understand how stressful it is to be a founder or CEO, managing
all the different elements of the company and bearing all the
responsibility for finances and growth.

My style as a founder CEO was to always beat myself up when
something went wrong. Therefore, it was incredibly helpful
for me to have board members who were good at supporting
and motivating. Often, they would tell me not to go so hard
on myself.

Of course, in some cases, depending on the temperament of
the CEO, the opposite approach may be required: if the person
is getting defensive, board members may need to deliver some
tough love. In my case, however, everyone could see I was my
own worst critic—and it went a long way for me to have board
members who understood this aspect of my psyche.

**The last thing you want as a founder is to wind up with a real
tyrant on your board, someone who's just banging their fists
against the wall all the time**—unless, I suppose, that's motivating for you. Maybe it is. In my case, I guess I have a certain
level of baseline intensity, and I know enough about myself to
know I need people on my board who are a little more amica-
ble—or else my intensity will clash with their intensity, and it
will get ugly.

My Series A was co-led by Monashees and Kaszek. I had met with both Hernan and Nico, the two founders of Kaszek. I liked them both, but they asked me to decide which one of them I wanted to join my board. I opted for Nico, mainly because I felt he balanced me out well. I am a pretty intense person, and my read was that Hernan has a similarly high level of intensity. I liked Nico's calm demeanor. I don't think there was a wrong decision in that scenario, but I was happy with the decision I made.

Personalities aside, when you're selecting who you want on your board, it's important to remember that the board is going to change as time goes on. Board seats are one of the tools you'll use to negotiate when taking on capital.

Here's what I mean: in the early days of a company, it's the founder who controls the board. But after you raise a certain amount of capital—usually when you get past Series B—what happens is that the board becomes independently controlled *or* board/investor controlled.

Say you have two founders, and then you get a seed investor to join. Now, you have three people on your board. Then, as you raise additional capital in Series A, the number grows: there are the two founders, the seed investor, the Series A investor, and maybe an additional independent investor. That makes five board members.

As founder, you can use your board seats as leverage. Especially when you have a very competitive deal with lots of interest from different parties, you have the ability to *not* give the investor a board seat.

But whenever you take investment, it's a good opportunity to validate and negotiate who the fund puts on your board. Talk to other startups and get feedback from those founders about the board members assigned by the fund. An extremely experienced investor and board member can be a really positive signal to future investors.

Over time, venture-backed companies often become controlled by the board. But in the early stages, they're still owned by the founders, and investors generally don't outnumber the founders yet. So the founders still have a lot of power, and they should use it. (As an early-stage investor myself, it's a red flag when I see companies that are controlled by the investors. It's a bad sign, and it puts me off. I always want to invest in founder-led companies.)

Use your judgment and, again, get feedback from other founders about specific board members.

Finally, it's worth mentioning that there's something called an independent board member who is neither an investor nor a founder but someone you bring onto the board to help. Typically, independent board members or independent directors are people who fill some gap in your business. Either they have really strong industry expertise or they're a mentor. For example, we had a guy named Sam Lessin, who was the vice president of product at Facebook. We knew he was really good at product and could help us become more of a product organization. So we brought him on as an independent board member.

> An independent board member is one who is neither an investor nor a founder but rather an industry expert brought on to fill a particular gap.

FIRING PEOPLE FROM YOUR BOARD

In terms of our board, at the beginning, it was just me, my dad, one of my best friends, and my co-founder Thomas. Our board meetings were just the four of us. But then Greg Waldorf came into the mix. As discussed earlier, he had invested in a similar business and was extremely well-connected when it came to raising stage financing (growth capital). He had also been a CEO himself, with experience scaling a company.

When Greg invested, he did it on the condition that my dad and best friend would leave the board.

That, of course, was a little awkward. **Once people get on boards, it's pretty tough ego-wise to convince them to step off.** But Greg was absolutely right on this one. It was a hard conversation to have, not so much with my dad (he understood and didn't take it personally), but my friend was understandably pissed off at first.

It's a tough pill to swallow, to be removed from a board and not involved in any decision-making anymore. But it was the right thing to do: neither of them had any experience with startup boards.

Clearly, raising money from family and friends can be fraught. I advise you to think twice before having your cousin or uncle put money into your company. It worked out fine for me in the end, but it can definitely create unnecessary conflict, especially if they want to be involved deeper in the operation.

And even if they're not family or friends, having to fire advisors is rough. I know I had a few of them that I let hang around for a while when I should have just cut them loose. If you feel like an advisor is not helpful anymore, you need to politely let them go—and replace them with someone else. Once you find a really good advisor, the difference will be abundantly clear. You'll feel how much they care and how they can impact your business, just like Greg and Simon Baker did.

Again, Simon was someone with deep experience building the same kind of business in Australia. Whereas Greg's value was as a CEO coach who helped, for example, with recruiting, Simon was a fantastic guide when it came to operations and strategy.

Both were, and are, amazing mentors—and both were integral in making our great advisory board what it was.

When all is said and done, boards are tricky but can be incredibly valuable. They're not to be feared, but you have to take them very seriously. A bad board can hurt your business, but a good board can help immensely. It's all about finding the right people and constructing your board the right way.

Yes, it takes a significant investment of time and energy to get this piece *right*, but the benefits are most definitely worth it.

CHAPTER EIGHT

THE BUILDING BLOCKS OF YOUR COMPANY

There are countless business frameworks out there for how to structure your team, and while companies definitely do need structure, there's no one right way to organize your business. The reality is that you adapt based on your needs and priorities at any given moment. For example, Brian's company was constantly changing the way it structured its sales team. Viva Real had been so focused on sales early on (because they didn't have a lot of money) that they neglected product and engineering. It's almost always preferable to have one bona fide technical co-founder from the get-go. Recruiting a CTO down the road, which is what Brian had to do, is incredibly hard; if you are in this position, make sure to reserve significant equity for it. When Brian finally brought on some good people, the company swung the pendulum too far in the other direction, putting its engineers on a pedestal and inadvertently creating a kind of class divide within the organization. Here, the author reveals various mistakes he made with different departments around the way they were organized (like letting his begrudging attitude toward remote teams cause him to not manage them well).

As we talked about earlier in chapter three, it's almost always preferable—even though admittedly, we didn't follow this rule ourselves!—to have one co-founder who's a bona fide technical co-founder, someone with a real background in engineering. You want a person like this from the get-go; if not a founder, then at least someone who's part of the founding *team*. It just goes a long way toward solving problems and helping you avoid headaches later on.

Recruiting a CTO down the road is really hard.

In Latin America, filling this difficult position is perhaps becoming a little easier, just by virtue of having more successful companies there now—and by extension, more people with valuable experience scaling a business. But when I was starting out, there weren't a lot of people at all with that background because there simply hadn't been very many startup success stories yet in the region.

It's getting progressively easier. But you still have to be very mindful when it comes to this piece of the puzzle. For one thing, if you're trying to recruit a good CTO, you need to reserve significant equity for that. This is especially important if you're a single founder or if neither you nor your co-founder are technical. And equity is important when you're trying to recruit good people for *any* position in your company.

But the reason I'm focusing here on the CTO role is that with a tech-oriented company, product and engineering really have to be at the center of what you're building. Having the right person and the right team in place is fundamental—and getting this wrong can be a massive roadblock for your company.

> CTO is one of the hardest positions to fill. Best to start out
> with a technical co-founder who can become CTO. If you *have*
> to recruit one later on, make sure to reserve significant equity
> for it.

Not having a technical co-founder from the beginning was just one of many mistakes I made when it came to product and engineering. In our case, Thomas was always involved in the product, but in the early days, he also ran engineering—until finally, we were able to hire a CTO. Then, once we did, it soon became clear that this fellow wasn't the right cultural fit. He was from India, and there was just a big difference between how things were done in India versus Brazil or Colombia.

Meanwhile, this was all happening during a time when our team from Colombia was just migrating to Brazil. We only had a few people and desperately needed new blood; specifically, folks with engineering experience. But it was just incredibly hard (and expensive) in Brazil at the time to find people like that.

As I mentioned in chapter three, technology and engineering were *always* one of our weak spots at Viva Real from the beginning. We got off to a bad start by not having a CTO or full-on technical co-founder, and honestly, we just always struggled with that part of our business.

Then, when we finally got some good people, including a new CTO, I made a different kind of mistake: I put these product and engineering folks on a pedestal.

THE PEDESTAL PROBLEM WITH ENGINEERS

This happens in a lot of companies, and the problem is that

you wind up creating almost two separate classes of people within your organization. It's something you have to really be conscious of and try to avoid. As with all the lessons in this book, I hope you can learn from my mistakes.

Here's why it's so difficult and such a tough balance. On the one hand, you can't deny the importance of the CTO role. You've *got* to make sure you have the right person. This is something that a *lot* of startups struggle with because there's such a scarcity of really good prospects for this position—and it's one that can make a huge impact on your business. This is true for product and engineering in general. Resources are really hard to find, and the good talent are 10Xers who'll build incredible value for your company.

Like with any company, people get paid according to their value to the organization. So with people in engineering, it's not strange or unusual for a twenty-eight-year-old to earn more than a forty-year-old marketing executive.

That's just how it goes sometimes, and the reality is that it's very hard *not* to create this class distinction.

But at the same time, you really have to try to keep it under control. Companies go too far—and we were no exception—in trying to cater to and coddle their engineers, which can create resentment through an organization.

In our case, I can see now that it was a mistake early on to go to such lengths to make our engineers feel "special." Of course, in theory, it's always good to make your people feel special: it's certainly better than the opposite. But it becomes a problem when it starts to stir up office politics or cause internal conflict.

I see now that our approach *did* hurt the culture of our organization to a degree. I don't know if we could have avoided the problem entirely, but I wish I had gotten out in front of the issue a little more and asked how people were feeling before too much resentment built up.

What would have probably also helped is if we had put our engineers and tech people in front of our customers more.

This isn't so much an issue with the product people. They're already largely customer-facing: when you're building a product, naturally you have to talk to customers. This is true regardless of what kind of business you are or what you're building—whether complex enterprise software or a consumer marketplace. Even if you're a B2B2C business where, say, you're selling into real estate companies, and then you're also building a product for the consumers who are looking for the property. Yes, you may have different types of customers or users, but your product people are still always talking to those audiences.

Not so, however, with the engineering people who are building the software. All too often, they will become very disconnected from the customer. That's no good. When your engineers are never front and center with your consumers, again, it creates a weird mentality.

But it doesn't *have* to be like that. To a large degree, this issue can be avoided by simply giving more exposure to those engineering teams and having them interact with different departments. It's a net positive: it creates more empathy for what you're building and who you're building it for and is just a good rule of thumb generally in business to have everyone understand what everyone else does within the company.

It helps people be better team players.

> Good product engineering people are hard to find—but when
> you do, they can have a 10X impact and create incredible value
> for your company.

OTHER ISSUES WITH BUILDING AND RUNNING ENGINEERING TEAMS

Finally, as it relates to product and engineering, and the CTO role, in particular, we've already talked about how important it is that the person be not only great at giving guidance on technology but also managing people. That's the difference between a CTO and a VP of engineering. The former is basically the highest kind of executive, and their responsibilities go beyond just technical decision making.

Again, that's why the CTO role is so hard to fill. What you tend to find time and again is that you'll have someone who's really strong on the tech side but who just doesn't have the people skills—or vice versa.

There's no getting around it: this is one of the hardest parts as you scale your organization to build out.

For example, when Google was building out its engineering team, they famously assumed that management wasn't going to be that important for engineering. They believed, mistakenly, that the engineers would be able to self-govern. Luckily, they caught their mistake before they went too far down that path. Google is, of course, a very data-driven company, so they actually ran experiments on this—and found that even though engineers often give a lot of pushback on being managed and say they don't like having management, it really is necessary. Critical even.

Similarly, when it comes to engineering, it's common—and getting more popular all the time—to have remote teams. I believe this is what the future looks like. But it's harder to implement when your company doesn't start out with remote as part of your culture.

One of my close friends (and angel investors in Viva Real), serial entrepreneur Alex Torrenegra, has been a great inspiration for me on this topic and has been building remote companies for over a decade now. Today, he runs Torre, where I am also an investor. (Oh, and you may know him as Shark from Shark Tank Colombia!)

In 2020, when California went into coronavirus lockdown, I found myself, along with my wife and kids, sharing a house in Lake Tahoe with Alex, his wife Tania, and daughter Azul. I used the time together to learn everything I could from Alex about remote work.

I consider Torrenegra the king of remote work. He wrote an entire book on the subject: *Remoter: The Why-and-How Guide to Building Successful Remote Teams*—and he, along with a few others, have given me a lot of great guidance about how to incorporate remote into my next venture from day one. (More about my new company, Latitud, can be found at the end of the book.)

Through 2018 and 2019, I had been planning on starting a new company. I knew I wanted to build something that was again focused on Latin America, but I also knew that moving back to the region full-time was probably not in the cards. I wanted to be close to my family in California. So, for the first time ever, I started thinking seriously about building a remote-first company.

Today, that remote-first company, Latitud, is a reality, and although we still only have a small team, amazingly I've yet to meet half of the people I've hired. On the surface, that may sound strange, but the truth is it's all working quite well. The team has been very productive. And it's actually not the first time I've hired people without meeting them in person. In the early days of Viva Real, I did the same with Sasha Astafyeva, a key executive who I hired from the Ukraine.

I think this is going to become more and more common: not just hiring people without meeting them in person but remote work in general. Look, I still don't think that every startup can or should become a fully remote business. And you have to be careful when you hire people without meeting them in-person. I suggest starting with a contract to hire. Do a trial for a specific project and see how it works. It's not perfect; there are still challenges. But the reality is that **in today's world, you lose talent if you don't allow for remote.** There are a lot of good people out there who just don't want to have to uproot themselves. So you kind of *have* to do it—and done right, this arrangement can indeed work.

But only if you manage it well, which we didn't at Viva Real.

In the early days of that company, most of our team-management problems stemmed, frankly, from me as CEO not knowing how to run teams effectively. I just didn't have a lot of experience as a manager. I was learning on the job. Then, when we moved our headquarters from Bogota, Colombia, to Sao Paulo, Brazil, and pivoted to the new market, it meant having a remote office. We also experimented with having a few people work from home.

> Having a satellite office or a few engineers working from home does *not* make you a remote company.

Remote work is all the rage right now. But to be completely honest, even though I now see incredibly positive aspects of remote work, it took me a *long* time to come around to this understanding. I had to overcome many of my own biases around the topic. At Viva Real, I always felt like my hand was kind of forced into allowing for remotes. Philosophically, I had long been a skeptic and was particularly resistant to the idea of remote engineering teams. My thinking was that people really needed to be there in the mix.

I had a lot of debates with my team about it. Eventually, I relented but never really gave our remote team the support it needed. We just weren't ever fully successful in having a remote engineering team. We didn't know how to manage it, and maybe we didn't have the will to learn. Ultimately, the remote teams were not as productive as they could have been. And we probably lost out on some great talent because of that.

Every startup has its areas where it's strong and areas where it's not so strong. We were no different.

WHAT ABOUT THE OTHER PARTS OF YOUR ORGANIZATION?

There are countless business frameworks out there for how to structure your teams. For example, these days, you have the concept that's all the rage of "squads" where team members have cross-functional roles.

I agree with Ben Horowitz, who says that "Every single org chart for a company is bad." He's being a little facetious, but what he means is that any org chart is only good for a certain moment of time, based on what you need at that juncture.

The way I would put it is that **there's no one right way to organize a business, but companies definitely *do* need structure.** In other words, it's certainly important to *have* an org chart and for there to be a well thought out logic behind it. But you can never be wed to a particular structure. All structures have problems. When you change from one structure to another, you're just removing one problem and adding a new one. Which is fine: you just have to be clear on which problem you'd prefer to have. There's no perfect solution, no one right answer to the question of who should report to whom, and so on. It's all very fluid. What matters is that you have to always be adaptable.

All too often, organizations become dogmatic about how they should be organized. It's similar to what you see with programming languages. There are many engineers who obsess about specific types of programming languages being better than others, but the reality is that usually there are a bunch of different frameworks that will get the job done just fine. What worries me is when I have an engineer who is fixated on what language is used. Often, the reason they're so concerned is that they want to learn a particular language, so they insist on using it—but it's all about satisfying their own intellectual curiosity. They're putting their personal interest ahead of what's good for the company.

There's just no room for that kind of rigidity in a startup, whether with programming languages or with org charts. In terms of how we organize our teams at Viva Real, I know that we have had virtually every kind of structure possible at one point or another. Seriously, there were probably twenty different iterations or permutations. We just kept on shifting around internally. None of these arrangements were "perfect" or anything I would insist other companies emulate.

The reality is that you end up adapting to whatever your priorities are; you design your structure based on your needs at the given moment.

RAISING CAPITAL AND FINANCING

CHAPTER NINE

THE WHAT

Not all companies should be raising money. Venture capital is for when you have a really big, attractive market and a really big opportunity and you need to accelerate your growth to capture market share. Angel investors and angel syndicates can play a crucial role. Your angel investors should either be deep operators or have access to stage financing (or both). You should also have local angel investors in the country where you operate or plan to expand who understand the market there. There's a lot of mystery to the VC world, and it can be hugely helpful if you can first understand the fundamentals of how investors think, the motivations behind their behavior, and the economics around how they operate and make money (including the role of limited partners, fees, carry, pro rata, and how investing is a business of hits). It is also important to understand and be able to distinguish between the different kinds of funds, from micro VCs to seed funds to early-, mid-, and late-stage funds. Ultimately, raising funding is not in itself a cause for celebration: it just means you now have a ton more responsibility and other stakeholders to work with! Furthermore, says Brian, you must always remember these are your investors, not your friends, and you shouldn't get too emotionally involved. There will be difficult times ahead, and investors will inevitably become more difficult when your company is not doing well. The sign of a good investor is someone who remains calm during a storm. Finally, says Brian, don't get discouraged or think it's all over if an investor says no. There are all kinds of reasons that an investor might pass, and it's not personal. Validation from them isn't everything.

Angel investors can play a critical role for first-time entrepreneurs. What I did when I first got angel investors at Viva Real is that—after the initial FFF capital (Friends, Family, and Fools)—I went out and raised money from Simon Baker and Greg Waldorf. They co-led the round and brought on a few other people to help fill it out. We raised $1.1 million.

Again, there were two buckets of angel investors. One consisted of people like Greg. He had a bit more of a network in Silicon Valley and access to future stage financing (Series A, B, C investors). He also had a lot of experience being part of start-ups—and lent credibility that helped us with access to future investors.

The other bucket of angel investors were deep operators with specific sector knowledge. This included Simon Baker as well as Shaun Di Gregorio. They were investors who could help and give insight into the operation piece, with their hands-on experience scaling companies in the same sector. Both Simon and Shaun played a key role in scaling a business similar to Viva Real in Australia, so they deeply understood the opportunities and challenges of our business.

For a first-time entrepreneur trying to raise funds—and really, I would recommend this structure to anyone raising capital for a venture-backed company—it's good to have both types of angel investors. You get a combination of experience, credibility with other investors, and knowledge of how to build a team and recruit, as well as how to navigate the stage financing process downstream.

Nowadays, whenever I make an investment myself, I make sure to connect the company I'm investing in with other people who I think could be good investors. I do this because I'm familiar with a lot of the angel investors and funds, and I know what their appetite is for different opportunities.

It's worth mentioning that there also exists a denomination called *super angels*—typically people who have had an exit before and have been part of that process. Super angels may also manage investment funds that include capital provided by third parties and therefore be able to invest more than other angels.

> Your angel investors should either be deep operators or people with access to stage financing (or both).

Note of caution for founders: there are a few important protections you should be aware of when raising money in an angel round.

First, you must realize that whatever terms you get early on from investors will set a precedent for future rounds. It's helpful, therefore, to have by your side a few different people, again from both buckets, who can participate in the angel round and help you.

Think carefully about the terms you receive when you take on an investment. It's very likely that these will constitute a template for the future. Most angel rounds or seed rounds use a **convertible note or convertible equity (e.g., a SAFE)**. Access to these convertible investment documents is more available now.

When you're negotiating certain aspects of a term sheet (more on this in the following chapter), and you give up a lot of those items early on, all of your future investors are going to want the same terms. That's just how it is. But most angel investors are comfortable with a standard convertible note or the YC SAFE—and this is recommended for early-stage financing as it is quick and keeps your legal fees down.

If there's one thing I wish I had done differently in my angel rounds, it's that I should have used a **Special Purpose Vehicle** (SPV), usually structured as a Delaware LLC, to pool small investors. It was a big headache having to chase down all the signatures I needed. For my next company, I will definitely use an SPV. It makes the structure much more efficient. Honestly, I still don't see these being used very often, but I anticipate they will become more commonplace in Latin America in the coming years. The times I *have* seen an SPV are in late-stage companies when the company wants to centralize all the angels into one vehicle. For example, I was an angel investor in a company where there were many other tiny shareholders like me who had each put $10,000–$50,000 into the business. The CEO emailed us to explain how the SPV would work. He wrote:

> As we scale, to make the cap table more manageable, we are going to move all of the Angels into an LLC. As I'm sure you can imagine, chasing each of you for signatures each time we need a shareholder resolution is quite challenging. Do not fear, this structure will not be permitted to sell your shares without your consent (other than in a sale of the entire company or an IPO) nor will it prevent you from selling shares in future secondary offerings. In addition, the company will be covering the costs associated with the LLC. We will circulate signatures for your authorization

to move your shares at the same time we conclude this funding/
secondary round.

My friend Mauricio Feldman of Volanty recommends that
founders set up an offshore structure from day one of their
business. He says: "You can do it for pretty cheap and it just
sends a message that you are here to go big." I feel the same
way. Nowadays, as an investor, if I see that a company is
raising money through a local entity, I will almost always
pass. There are a number of reasons for an offshore structure,
including, primarily, liability protection, tax optimization,
clearer governance, investor familiarity, and more flexibility
on an exit.

HOW TO FIND AN ANGEL INVESTOR

I would also recommend finding angel investors from local
markets. People who understand your market. You don't just
want to get some random person who has no connection with
your country or your industry. They don't add any weight. With
someone like that, all it really shows is that you got some rich
person to invest money.

But when you're able to get a local expert or someone with
domain experience or local knowledge, it carries a real punch.
It brings credibility.

With my own fundraising, when I went out and raised money,
I went to a bunch of local investors. In addition to Simon and
Greg, I had a few other angel investors like Micky and Wences,
the legendary entrepreneurs and investors who founded and
sold Patagon Bank to Santander and Lemon Bank to Banco
do Brasil. But even with my local angel investors, almost all of

them were in one of those two buckets: either they were deep operators, or they had access to stage financing.

How did I end up getting these people on board? Typically, it starts with a lead investor. In my case, I had already brought in Simon: his experience lent credibility, and this gave Greg more comfort to invest. Then, once Greg committed, he went out and helped me line up an additional $750,000 from contacts he had. This was basically what you would call today an **angel syndicate.**

An angel syndicate is a VC fund created to make a single investment. They are led by experienced technology investors and financed by institutional investors and sophisticated angels.

In the US, it is common for these lead investors to make an investment and then line up additional capital from their syndicate or network. In some cases, they charge carried interest of 20 percent on the investment. Let's say that I made an investment of $50,000 into a company. I also helped line up another $1 million. As the lead of the syndicate, I would get 20 percent of the profits that are returned from the investment. So if the $1 million invested returned $10 million in profit, I would be compensated $2 million in carried interest for finding, diligencing, and negotiating the terms of the deal.

Again, this is where I believe SPVs will soon come more into play. This model is indeed becoming more popular, but when I raised my angel round, it wasn't common. Both Simon and Greg negotiated some additional equity (2 percent vested over time) as part of their investment in the form of an advisor agreement, which is something you see more often. It was a lot of equity to give up, but in my case, it proved to be worth it. It was my first time running a venture-backed company, and both Simon and Greg helped quite a bit.

Aside from the SPV model, I predict the growth of rolling funds over the coming years. A **rolling fund** is a new type of investment vehicle that allows its managers (so far, mostly founders) to share deal flow with fund investors on a quarterly subscription basis while netting carried interest over a multi-year period (e.g., two to four years).

A rolling fund is structured as a series of limited partnerships: at the end of each quarterly investment period, a new fund is offered on substantially the same terms, for as long as the rolling fund continues to operate. With this fund structure, rolling funds are publicly marketable and remain open to new investors. (Hence the term "rolling.")

This book won't go into the future of venture capital, but it is my belief that rolling funds are the start of software beginning to eat away at the traditional venture model. I think this is the natural evolution of founders becoming investors, and it lets you get started with a lot less friction and initial set-up costs. Creating a formal venture fund from scratch can cost between $50k–$100k, and it is expensive to maintain. I believe this will open up access to more diverse fund managers kicking off a new wave of "Solo Capitalists."

Founders want to receive investment from other founders—people who have been in their shoes and can speak to the challenges they are facing—and angel investing has blurred the lines between investor and advisor. I am a big fan of founders raising money from other founders in the early days. As Latin America's startup ecosystem continues to grow, this trend will continue. Instead of people talking about the PayPal mafia, we'll hear about the Nubank, Konfio, Quinto Andar, and Cornershop mafias (along with dozens of other companies that have built tremendous value). I hope all of the founders of these companies and others raise funds to reinvest back in the ecosystem.

Maybe you are next in line?

HOW DO YOU KNOW IF *YOU* SHOULD BE RAISING MONEY?

As a founder, how do you determine if venture capital is even applicable to your business?

Not all companies should raise venture capital.

For example, service businesses like, say, advertising agencies are typically *not* well-suited for venture capital. They just don't have that same scalability that software companies do.

Similarly, businesses that are highly dependent on consultants are probably not well-suited to take on venture capital either. The exception to that rule is if the business is itself a marketplace for consultants—like what Upwork does for the freelance market, connecting people from all over the world and helping them come together. (Something like that is really more of a "network effects marketplace." This refers to a phenomenon whereby a product or service gains additional value as more people use it.) But if you're a local company that's reliant on consultants and you don't have a model that's going to scale to a certain size, you should not be raising money.

So when *should* you be looking to raise venture capital?

If you know you've got a very large market or TAM (Total Addressable Market) and you really need to accelerate your growth to capture market share—after all, *someone* is going to have market share—then venture capital makes a lot of sense. You need that push, those additional resources, to be able to grow fast and attract the best people.

In short, venture capital is for when there's a really big attractive market and a really big, billion-dollar opportunity. A good example would be a startup that has a great piece of bookkeeping software that does something totally different and helps small businesses in a game-changing way. The small-business market in Latin America is a really big market. There are hundreds of thousands of small businesses, and many of these are still using Excel to manage their finances. So, to stick with this example, here you are with this great software solution for these small businesses. But you're stuck because in order to scale the products, you need to hire more salespeople and engineers. You need to invest in marketing so you can get your message across and onboard more customers. You need customer success people to make sure customers are using the software appropriately. It's a lot!

Now, keep in mind: paying for all that stuff in your business may not allow for profitability initially. You may not be profitable for five years. But if you've proven that you can sign up x amount of customers, it's absolutely worth it—to you and to VCs.

There's a concept you're probably familiar with called **LTV Over CAC**, which means Lifetime Value of a Customer over Customer Acquisition Costs. The LTV:CAC ratio measures the relationship between the lifetime value of a customer and the cost of acquiring that customer. The ratio is divided into two components: customer lifetime value and customer acquisition cost.

Customer Lifetime Value indicates how long an average customer sticks with you before they stop paying and the value they generate throughout this cycle. Generally, the longer a customer stays with you, the more valuable they are. Customer Acquisition Cost shows how much it costs you to acquire a new customer on average. Most of the time, it costs more to acquire a new customer than to keep an existing one.

In numbers:

LTV = Average spending in X amount of time * How many times "X amount of time" repeats itself within average time spent as a client

E.g., clients' average spending = $2,000/month, average time spent as client = 24 months, LTV = $2,000*24 = $48,000

CAC = cost of marketing and sales efforts for all clients in X amount of time (including payroll, commission, ads, graphic materials, CRM etc.) / customers acquired in that X amount of time

E.g., total expenditure on marketing and sales in 24 months = $480,000, number of customers acquired in 24 months = 60, CAC = $480,000/60 = $8,000

In this made-up example: if your company's LTV is $48,000 and the total cost of acquiring a customer is $8,000, then your LTV:CAC ratio is 6:1.

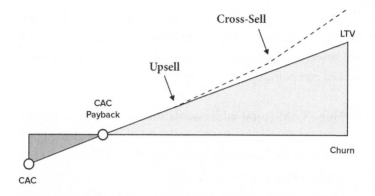

The point is: there's a high probability the customer is going to stay with you. You've got low churn—the customer likes your product and wants to stick with you—but also the switching costs are really high. If another software provider were to come in and offer the same, it would be expensive for the user. They would have to retrain their team and adapt to a new process.

If you are serving them well and anticipating the needs of your customer, you can stay out in front. **The high switching cost creates a "moat" around your business.**

Clearly, a business in a large market with an LTV:CAC ratio like that is one that should be venture-backed. The capital will help them get the needed talent. Maybe it will even allow them to acquire other businesses—or eventually go public (in which case they'll need the strong connections and expertise that the VC provides them).

A HELPFUL FRAMEWORK FOR THINKING ABOUT FUNDRAISING

There's a very useful framework that my friend and fellow entrepreneur, Mauricio Feldman—along with his Volanty co-founder,

Antonio Avellar—came up with. It's essentially a playbook for how to think about fundraising when building a startup, and it is based on the following five important criteria for venture-backed companies:

1. **Huge TAM (total addressable market).** Go after the big markets, focusing on the ones that are the most challenging, that have the biggest inefficiencies. This will help you raise capital. You will still make mistakes, but in large markets like this, you have nine lives because you are able to typically raise significant cash—giving you more opportunities to find the right solution for the market

2. **Technology that is not widely used.** This has evolved a lot, but the fact remains that traditional industries are not good at using tech at scale. In building your venture-based company, you don't have to reinvent the wheel. You can take technology that already exists and apply it to a market that doesn't have strong tech. To quote my friend David Vélez, whereas most banks see themselves as financial services companies that happen to use technology, "Nubank is a tech company that happens to offer financial services." It may seem like a subtle distinction, but it makes a huge difference.

3. **Revenue from Day Zero.** The reason this is important is the same reason that I don't like to invest in social networks— you need millions of users before you can make any money, and in most cases, you don't have a local competitive advantage, so you are competing with global players.

4. **Foreign benchmarks.** Using an international proxy—e.g., "Volanty is the Brazilian Vroom"—helps global investors understand your business better. Yes, you should focus on solving specific local problems and will likely need to tropicalize the solution to address a unique market need. But using foreign benchmarks is still important in helping

you reach investors and articulating to them what you are building.

5. **Clear pain**. When it comes to the problem that your company is solving, make sure that the pain is severe and common, something that the VC can identify with. A great test for this is if you are sitting around having a beer with ten friends and you tell them you have to sell your car and all of them react negatively because they know it isn't a fun process, you are seeing a clear pain. The opposite of this would be don't look for a problem that isn't there. Having a clear pain that is obvious to everyone makes it so much easier to talk to potential recruits, investors, and the media.

Mauricio told me that, if he had built that framework today, he would have probably added another two important criteria: unit economics and CAC under control. That being said, if your company satisfies the five criteria above, you are likely well-positioned to raise venture capital. There are all kinds of reasons why venture capital is a good look for founders like you. Assuming you came to this book because either a.) you are already a venture-backed startup or b.) you know you need to become one in order to expand and capture the market share you require, then you should be paying special attention to this chapter. The reality is: there's a lot of mystery to the world of venture capital. My advice is to first make sure you understand the fundamentals of how the investors think, the motivations behind their behavior.

If you want to understand how *you're* going to raise money, first you need to get a grasp on how VCs make money themselves.

HOW VCS WORK

A lot of folks in the startup world don't really think about venture capital from the VC standpoint. It may sound obvious, but **VCs have to raise money too.** Here you are, as a founder, out trying to raise money for your business, talking to these funds to try to get *them* to invest. But you've got to remember they're also trying to raise money themselves and generate a return for their investors! When you're fundraising, you will be in a much better position—empowered to make smarter choices—if you can understand the dynamics and incentives on the VC's end, what their financial model is, and how they operate.

First of all, how do they get paid?

Traditionally, VCs make their money based on how much they are able to raise when they go out and pitch to what are called *limited partners,* or LPs, who commit to investing capital into their fund. This LP group is made up of a mixture of investors. They can include endowments, corporate pension funds, sovereign wealth funds, wealthy families, and "fund of funds."

Then, within the VC itself, usually you've got the general partners or GPs, who are the people who manage the fund. You also have Principals, Associates, Analysts, Venture Partners, and an EIR (Entrepreneur In Residence). The first two just refer to the seniority of the team member. As for Venture Partners, they're the folks who help out temporarily with investments and management. Finally, an EIR is an entrepreneur looking for his or her next business opportunity.

Once the VC raises the money for a fund—let's say $100 million—that money is now committed and allocated for the fund.

So how then do all the people within the VC actually make their money?

First, you have what's called the *management fee,* which is typically 2.5 percent of the total capital allocated to the fund. With a $100 million fund, that would be $2.5 million annually. It's the money used to run the fund, pay the salaries of the team, invest in travel, and any other auxiliary expenses.

But where VCs really make their money is on what's called *the carry.* If we continue with the example of the fund that's raised $100 million, let's now imagine that all of the investments out of that fund have generated a total return of $300 million. In that case, a $100 million would go back to the investors, but then the fund operators or GPs would typically make 20 percent of the carry—and here the carry would be calculated on the $200 million profit. So the partners (and maybe some of the associates who had some kind of incentive) would wind up making $40 million on the carry.

To be honest, even though this is how it works and how VCs make the majority of their money, I don't think the management fees model is optimal. The problem with it, in my opinion, is that some VCs try to raise large funds just to collect as much money as possible from these fees. Long term, I think this structure may change. But until a better model comes along, it's just how the world works.

Of course, when a fund deploys capital, it also needs to make sure its investments go well. The goal for the VC is to increase the value of those investments so that they can raise their next fund. Which brings us to the third and final way that VCs help optimize their returns, which is using what's called *pro rata.*

The life of a fund is anywhere from seven to ten years. What usually happens is the VC takes that $100 million they raised for the fund and reserves 40–60 percent of it for "follow-on investments" (i.e., they don't include that money in the initial investments). Then, as a portfolio company raises additional rounds of capital, typically the fund reserves part of that money to keep its equity stake through a *pro rata*.

Another important element is that early-stage VCs place a large number of "small bets" on companies. Then, later, when they see which ones are having success, they use their pro rata rights to put more money to work in those companies. It's a way for them to manage risk. More of their money goes to the best companies.

Think of it like this: if someone buys 20 percent of a company, the founders own 80 percent. But then if another round of investment comes in and someone else buys 20 percent, those earlier investors who owned 20 percent are now diluted by 20 percent and only own 16 percent. Of course, the founders' equity is also diluted. Pro rata gives the investors that now own 16 percent the right to invest the amount equivalent to those 4 percent in that round, so they are back to owning 20 percent.

As a founder, you have to **be okay with owning a smaller piece of a bigger pie.** Granted, this is something I had a hard time coming to grips with myself. When we started Viva Real, Thomas and I owned the company. Then, we got a few angel investors and had to ask ourselves, did we want to continue owning and controlling most of the business? These are tough questions.

With the VCs, however, it's pretty clear: they don't want to see their equity diluted with additional rounds of investment. So what tends to happen—especially when it's a really attractive investment—is that most investors will want to keep *pro rata*, reserving part of their funds for follow-on capital.

§ VCs use *pro rata* to help maintain their stake in great companies. §

As a founder, this is all very important for you to know and understand. With any VC that you are potentially getting involved with, you should always take a close look and ask questions. What's the status of their fund? How much capital do they have left in their fund? Are they going to have money for follow-on investments? Are they just starting their fund? Have they got the capital committed yet in their fund? Asking these questions sends a positive signal that you understand this world. Good investors will answer the questions openly and confidently.

A lot of founders don't realize this, but **investors may look at investing in your company *before* they've actually circled up the capital.** Especially with a newer fund—maybe a first-time fund for some fund managers—they're on the hunt for companies that can show they have good access to deals. This allows them to go raise money from LPs. This is why it is important to understand the status of the fund: you don't want to have to wait for the VC to circle up the cash to invest in you.

Another surprising aspect of the VC world that most people aren't aware of is how the returns are so concentrated. If there are 25 portfolio companies in a fund, 80–90 percent of the VC returns will likely come from just one or maybe two of the top companies.

Many VCs don't actually make strong returns. It's a hard game to be good at. Most of the companies in a VC's portfolio aren't wildly successful either, but a few are, and that's how they pay the bills. It's **a business of hits**. For investors, their return comes like this: if they put $100 million in twenty-five investments, then out of those twenty-five, five are likely to shit the bed, and fifteen are just zombie companies that never make any money.

It's those remaining five investments that have to do all the work and more, but usually, it comes down to one or maybe two big winners.

It also depends on what stage the investor comes in at. Those numbers are assuming that they came in at Series A. If it is a seed fund, however, it might look even worse. Later-stage VCs have less risk, but multiples are lower.

WHAT DO VCS LOOK FOR IN A COMPANY?

The psychology of VCs is really fascinating. When pitching to a VC, a company may seem to have everything going for it—a really interesting business that's growing nicely—but the VC may still determine that the size of the market is too small for the business to ever become a billion-dollar company.

In order for the economics to work for a VC, the VC needs to have a thesis: that there's a way the company can become really large. The reason this is essential for VCs is simple mathematics: as we've seen, probability and past experience show that not every one of their investments is going to work out. Far from it. So with every investment they make, their mindset always has to be that this one will cover the other investments.

It makes sense, but it means **there are often great businesses out**

there that get passed over by VCs simply because they don't have the perceived ability to ever grow big enough.

VCs are also looking for different qualities in a company based on whatever stage the company is in. For example, when they are looking at an early-stage company, *team* is very important. But then at Series B, *traction* and *growth* become the name of the game.

Now that I am an investor myself, I understand so much better how VCs look at companies and make decisions about whether or not to invest in them. I know that I only invest in businesses that I really *understand*, and ones where I can see ways to help. Of course, I also have to be convinced that they can be a true leader in the market where they operate.

I also look for companies that are successfully resolving local friction points. By this, I mean ones that can only be successful if the team operates out of Latin America and builds the business within that region. Of course, after you become a market leader in Brazil or Mexico, and you're very successful, you can look at expanding into Europe or the US or anywhere else. As an investor, I would be delighted to see that and be a part of it. But initially, I need to see that you can win in your market. That's what you always need to prove.

I bring this up to help give you some insight into the minds of investors and the kinds of business models that they—and I— like to invest in. For example, I invest in a lot of marketplaces and platforms very much like Viva Real, companies whose business model depends on them having access to, or direct contact with, their clients (in VR's case, brokers and agents). For founders who are sitting in Silicon Valley or New York, it's much harder to build a business like that.

Take, for instance, fintech companies. By definition, these are very local in every dimension. There are tons of processes and integrations that are set up exclusively with local partners, not to mention a lot of local regulatory issues that they need to understand and comply with.

Fintechs are way more appealing for investment than, say, a social network or a search engine. With businesses like that, it's pure technology and you can do it from anywhere in the world. Any time I see a pitch from someone trying to create a social network in Brazil, it gets passed on. How can you build a defensible business like this against players who are big in the same area somewhere else?

In my conversations with Nico Szekasy from Kaszek, he states, "We *are* drawn to companies that do things like payroll process or tax accounting because those tend to be very local in nature. In contrast, if someone wants to build, say, a productivity tool, it doesn't interest us much—it's just too hard to see how they're going to compete with a team building the same thing somewhere else."

> When it comes to Latin America, VCs are looking to invest in the kinds of companies that can win the *region*—and don't have to compete against players around the world.

If you're trying to understand the psychology of VCs and what they're looking to invest in, obviously it also helps to look at what they're already invested in. Founders will take a peek at a particular fund and see that they're invested in MercadoLibre or Nubank and conclude that the fund must be good. This is a smart approach. But for better or worse, it also feeds into something called the *virtuous cycle*, which refers to how the best funds that are in all the best deals tend to attract the best founders.

The issue there is just in how it creates a kind of self-fulfilling prophecy effect: great investments attract more and better investments—which is how VCs are able to get the best deals.

The virtuous cycle can be a good and bad thing, depending on where you fall in the hierarchy. But no matter who you are, you have the right and ability to look closely at the funds and assess them just like they're assessing you.

Especially in cases where an investor is competing for a deal, and there are multiple interested investors in a company, founders can and do often dig into the track record of a particular fund. They may see that the investor was part of a certain deal with a company that's very successful, and that knowledge can definitely influence who the founder takes money from. Then, when the company is looking to raise more capital down the road—or even attract employees—people will see that this or that fund invested in their business. It becomes a seal of approval.

Finally, when new investors come in—after the early-stage investors, there are Series A, B, and C growth investors who invest later—there's a bit of a positive bias effect if a top fund has already invested in you. It serves as a signal to other funds that you're the real thing.

So do your homework **and look at the track record of the fund to see who they have invested in before.** When it comes to pitching VCs, doing your research is a crucial part of the process.

Knowledge is power, and now that you understand the financial model for how these funds operate and make money, it's important that you also educate yourself around the different types of venture capital.

TYPES OF FUNDS

Let's run down these, one by one.

After your angel investors, which we've already discussed, you have what's called a *micro VC*, which is usually a very small seed fund. In Latin America, a micro VC would probably be $5 million to $15 million. This is for the seed capital that goes into a business in its early stages (pre-seed and seed), and a **lot of these micro VCs are created and run by former entrepreneurs who had an exit and then made angel investments.**

Next, there are *seed funds*, which in Latin America can be anywhere from $10 to 50 million. These are typically invested in seed rounds and occasionally in Series A. Usually, they're first institutional money in or early capital. Then, after investing in a seed round, maybe they do their pro rata—and occasionally creep up to a Series A round.

After that, there are what we call *early-stage funds*, which are typically Series A funds (on occasion, they'll do Series B).

Then, there are *mid-stage funds*, which are also referred to as "growth investors."

Finally, there are the *late-stage funds*, which really can be better described as pre-IPO investors, often hedge funds or private or growth equity funds. This is a corner of the fund ecosystem that has seen a lot of convergence in recent years as late-stage investors move earlier in the investment life cycle and early-stage investors raise larger funds (as noted above) to do later-stage deals.

Those are the different funds broken down in terms of their fund sizes, i.e., the overall pie they have to use. But what about the check sizes or the amount of money they will typically invest in an individual company?

In Micro VCs, checks can be anywhere from $50,000 to $500,000. Seed investment is anywhere from $500,000 to $1.5 or $2 million. Mid-stage funds and late-stage funds, for their part, usually write larger checks. There are always outliers for all the different stages.

How Startup Funding Works

How Much You Get and How You Get it

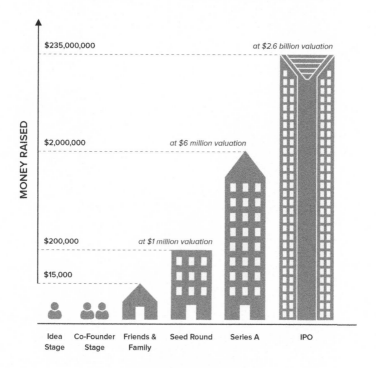

How Startup Funding Works

Splitting Up the Pie

Idea Stage	Co-Founder Stage	Friends & Family	Seed Round	Series A–D*	IPO
• Founder	• Founder 1	• Founder 1	• Founder 1	• Founder 1	• Founder 1
	• Founder 2	• Founder 2	• Founder 2	• Founder 2	• Founder 2
		• Uncle	• Uncle	• Uncle	• Uncle
		• Option Pool	• Option Pool	• Option Pool	• Option Pool
			• Angel	• Angels	• Angels
				• VCs	• VCs
					• Public

Typically, multiple financing happens before an IPO.

What Everyone Does

You	Start the company.
Co-Founder	Does half of the work.
Friends & Family	Invest before anyone else at the lowest price.
Angel Investors	Have at least $1,000,000 or earn $200,000 annually—are accredited investors. Invest their own money.
Venture Capitalists	Persuade other people to put money in their fund. Invest that money starting at $500,000.
Early Employees	Gamble on your company by accepting low salaries plus some stock.
Investment Bankers	Do IPO paperwork and sell a lot of your stock, getting 6–8 percent of the whole IPO for it.
Anyone	After your company does the IPO, anyone in the world can become your investor.

Those are the categories of funds within a venture ecosystem.

But what about international investors?

INTERNATIONAL INVESTORS

Most international investors who look at Latin America are from the US and Europe, with more recent interest from Asia, particularly China. These international investors kind of hang

on the sidelines and wait to see what local investors are investing in.

For an institutional investor—someone sitting at their desk
in Silicon Valley, on Sand Hill Road, or somewhere in Man-
hattan—chances are they have very few investments in Latin
America. They're much more likely, therefore, to take a cue from
a local investor like Monashees and Kaszek (full disclosure: both
invested in my Series A round).

Most institutional investors also look to follow on to not just
any local fund but the *best* ones, with the strongest reputa-
tions. That's how the flow generally works. But not always. For
example, Andreessen Horowitz (also known as a16z) has done
a few investments in Latin America without any local investors.
After that, everyone else wanted to jump on the bandwagon,
because a16z has such an amazing reputation. Which, as we've
seen, is **the allure of having a top-tier fund: it adds credibility
to your business.**

Certainly, most Series B and C capital comes internationally.
There's just not a strong enough ecosystem yet in Latin America to support growth capital, but this is starting to change fast.
While growth capital still comes predominantly from the US,
in the coming years, I believe we will see more growth funds
popping up in Latin America and heavier investments from
China, as evidenced by Didi acquiring 99.

Typically, international investors like to co-invest with or follow
a local investor.

YOUR PSYCHOLOGY AROUND RAISING CAPITAL—
AND AROUND YOUR INVESTORS

Say you're a founder who's just raised your first capital. Good for you! What I would tell you is, "Congrats: the real work starts now." **People like to celebrate fundraising, but it really just means you now have a shitload more responsibility.** The pressure has ratcheted up, and you are on the hook to actually deliver those results.

When we got our first outside money, I asked Thomas how he wanted to celebrate. His answer: McDonald's. I almost never eat McDonald's, but I made an exception that day. That's right: we ended up celebrating our funding over Big Macs. I am glad we didn't go crazy with champagne and cigars. That kind of celebration is way premature. The truth is that when you're starting out and you get your first funding, it's less a cause for celebration and more a wake-up call. What it really means is that all the work is *ahead* of you.

I don't say this to be a grinch or hater. It's cool to pat yourself on the back for a second, but it should really only be a second, and then you should get back to work—because you've got a *lot* of stuff in front of you now.

⸙ Just got your first funding? Congrats: the real work starts now! ⸙

As for your new investors, I would encourage you to always remember they are your investors, *not your friends.* **Don't get too emotionally involved with your investors.** It's easy to get it twisted. I've seen it time and again: when you're the hot company, you get all the love and attention from the VCs. They treat you amazingly, and it can be nice. But you have to remember that your relationship is heavily contingent on how well your business is doing. If your business isn't going well, you can expect your relationship with your investors to be rockier. I am thankful that, in some cases, I developed some real friendships with my investors, but this is not the default.

What makes you the darling in any moment is how promising you are or how successful. It's either a.) the hope that you're going to be really big because you're performing really well and getting bigger, or b.) you're already really big and therefore valuable to your investors.

In both scenarios, everyone's happy. The founder and the investor. What I've come to realize, however, is that **where the best investors show their greatness is in how they behave in hard times.**

As an investor myself, what I always try to achieve is not letting my emotions get the best of me. I remember that, however I'm feeling, the founder is almost certainly feeling worse and having an even harder time.

Of course, when a founder's business (who I've invested in) is struggling, naturally, I'm disappointed too. It's not fun for anyone. But it helps to have been on both sides of that situation. For example, I had an investor who ended up putting money into Viva Real in November 2014 and you probably remember, this just happened to be during a period when the US dollar was crushing the Brazilian *real*. This guy invested thirty million *dollars* (the total amount in the round was $41.3 million), and the investment was great for the company because we had it in dollars. By holding onto it in dollars and eventually moving it into Brazilian *reais*, we dramatically increased our money. But it also affected this investor's return for the worse. The company was valued in dollars at the time of the investment based on our growth and revenue in *reais*. When the *real* began to weaken, this resulted in our revenue (when calculated in dollars) decreasing. There was a several-year period where the currency eroded the increased revenue we produced in *reais*. In the end, despite the business growing in *reais*, the total dollar value didn't really increase. The investor was understandably disappointed—but trying to time currency fluctuations is impossible.

The timing was off. But the currency issue was just part of it. Truth is, we hadn't performed incredibly well. If we had over-performed, we could have compensated for the *real* being weak and increased the value of the company. Unfortunately, over the five-year period that this investor had his money in, that's not what happened. Instead, our company's value stayed around the same level.

If he had been a newer investor who wasn't as experienced, he might have reacted more emotionally—because he'd be worried about raising his next fund.

This is also why earlier stage funds that are not well-established feel pressure to mark up their investments—which can be a real problem for a founder. Raising all that money might seem like a good thing at first but ultimately can create complications for a business.

It's a bit of a broken system, honestly.

As you'll remember, the way it works is that investors usually raise their first fund based on the potential of their first investments. The second fund is typically more about how their companies are actually doing. But at this point, in their second fund, an investor usually hasn't had any exits yet. And they can only raise their third fund *if* they've had some exits or they have a few extremely promising companies in their portfolio.

Long story short: when the businesses they're investing in aren't doing very well, it can be very emotional for the investor—because they're not able to raise more money. Instead, they fizz out.

Luckily, with the investor who took a hit because of the weak local currency, this wasn't his first rodeo, so he was able to keep a good perspective and not react emotionally.

Nonetheless, it's important to remember that *all* **investors will become more difficult when your company is not doing well.**

The sign of a good investor is someone who remains calm during a storm.

I know founders who have had some pretty bad experiences with investors. As mentioned in chapter seven, the investors will show up to board meetings and be on their phone or not listening. Even though these people don't know much about the business, they try to sound like they do and put on an annoying and unwelcome performance to seem smart.

Fortunately, I've seen very little of this kind of behavior in my own relationships with investors. I've actually had really good investors all along and have been very happy with them for the most part.

Nonetheless, having been around the proverbial block a few times now, I've seen that as a group—this is not true of all but a lot of them—many investors don't have a lot of independent thinking. They tend to behave a little like sheep. They're very momentum-oriented: wanting to know who else is investing in your company so that they can jump on the bandwagon and ride the perceived momentum.

The best investors, however, develop their own thesis and stick with it. Sometimes they might miss a deal because it doesn't fit within what they believe, but it allows them to develop more discipline because they have clarity around the type of company, founder, or market that they prioritize.

But few investors have that kind of self-awareness. They don't generally have their own take on things. I say this not to beat up on them. I am now an investor myself, and I see how hard it is. Investors are very much tied to their *own* investors (LPs) and always need to justify the investments they make. In this context, it's understandable not to want to stick your neck out— but the best investors do.

I remember way back when I was trying to raise capital myself with an SF-based hedge fund. I talked to thirty investors, and they all said no. But what I took from that experience ulti-mately—and this is a lesson that I now try to impart on founders all the time—is that **investors really don't know everything**.

It's not that these thirty investors were wrong to reject us. Yes, we had a business that was interesting, but a lot of investors just didn't believe we were capable of making it happen. That, or they didn't see the market opportunity.

And here's what's important—it's *okay* that they didn't see it.

A lot of investors didn't see Airbnb for many years. They passed on it because it just didn't make sense to them. That's the real lesson here. **Validation from investors isn't everything.** Yes, it's important for speed. But your *customers* also provide validation by buying your product—which, in turn, provides validation for investors.

There are all kinds of reasons an investor might say no to you. It could just have to do with the timing of their fund. Or yes, it could be that they're really not interested or haven't seen what they need to see in you and your idea yet. Maybe they want to wait until you show more progress. Maybe they need you to build a stronger team.

> Just because an investor says no, don't get discouraged and think it's all over.

With every rejection, you're learning more and more about the VC world and how to best position yourself to get the funding you need. Fundraising is an iterative process where you learn from every pitch you do. You constantly evolve your pitch and refine your messaging.

In the following chapter, you're going to learn how to go in prepared to negotiate the best deal.

CHAPTER TEN

THE HOW

One of the most important parts of fundraising has to do with understanding negotiating your term sheet. The term sheet is the blueprint for your business in terms of future financing and your relationship with the investor. But the first time Brian got one, he didn't even know what the terms meant. He had to look them up on Wikipedia! Now, he's determined to help readers know the key areas you need to pay close attention to—namely, economics and control—while not sweating all the small stuff like he did. Brian walks readers through everything you need to know about valuation and term sheets: from how valuation is determined to how to calculate your runway (and the perils of having to do a down round); from pre-money versus post-money to employee option pools (and vesting); from liquidation preferences to drag-along rights; and more. Finally, he explains how deal heat and FOMO drive valuation and gives readers lots of helpful tricks of the trade for your interactions with VCs, from leveraging the power of social proof to using YC deck templates for your presentations.

As mentioned in the Introduction, the first time I got a term sheet, I didn't even know what any of the terms meant. I had to go to Wikipedia to look them up! That's how much of a novice I was.

But I did know that the term sheet was *important.*

Your "term sheet" is the blueprint for your business in terms of future financing and your relationship with the investor. It lays out the critical terms of the documentation and explains how the deal is going to work. While it's not legally binding until adapted into a proper contract by a lawyer—people can, but rarely do walk away from deals before final docs are signed— obviously, the term sheet is still a big deal and not something to screw up!

My problem was I had no clue what was actually in it. What were the most important parts, the key terms I should be negotiating? I had no idea, and my anxiety was through the roof. I showed the term sheet to a friend who was a junior lawyer at the time. He helped as best he could, but mostly it was just me agonizing and spending countless hours, unnecessarily, researching each term and sweating a bunch of stuff I really didn't need to be worrying about.

I remember obsessing over "registration rights," "conditions precedent to financing," and "information rights." Eventually, I discovered that these were insignificant, nothing more than your average contract jargon—but at the time, they sounded so scary!

For example, I can't tell you how much I freaked out over "registration rights." What does that even mean, you ask? It's almost not worth explaining: in the United States, you have to register a sale of shares with the SEC in order for them to become liquid and be freely tradable. Only the company can make that registration. Registration rights just refer to investors' right to require the company to register their shares in an IPO or afterward when there is a public market for shares. But it almost goes without saying. It's a completely standard, boring part of the process—locking up the shares in an IPO and giving investors certain rights to determine an IPO of a company—but something you'll find in every single term sheet (and almost never exercised in practice).

Look, there's nothing wrong with learning about things like registration rights—if that's what floats your boat (each to their own!)—but don't lose sleep over them.

When it comes to term sheets, there are really two key areas you need to concern yourself with: **economics** and **control**.

THE TERM SHEET: ECONOMICS

What investors care about most—and you should too—is the economics, meaning how much money is being invested and at what valuation.

Let's talk, first, about valuation. How is it even determined in the first place? There are multiple factors, but it's heavily dependent on the stage of the company. A mature company would determine valuation by doing discounted cash flows and coming up with a model like a multiple-on-profit or EBITDA.

With an early-stage company, there's really no equation at all: your valuation is dependent on how many people want to invest, how experienced the entrepreneurs are, how good the team, and how big the market and overall opportunity.

Typically, it's the founder who will initially try to define the price. You'll remember that when I first approached Simon as an investor, he walked out on me. This was because I was trying to raise $1 million at a $6 million valuation—and he wasn't seeing it.

I crapped out that day. But you never know. For example, Loft in Brazil raised $18 million out of the gate like it was nothing, based on a PowerPoint presentation. They knew it was aggressive but also knew they *needed* that level of funding. Because they're in real estate, and their business involves buying real estate, their whole premise requires a lot of capital. Given these parameters, the founders Mate and Florian knew they had to be aggressive in their asks—and the plan worked for them. They both also happen to be second-time founders, which helps with credibility, and some of the best executors in Brazil.

Of course, the trick is not to go so far that the investor walks away, like Simon did with me at first, or set yourself up for failure down the road. You have to figure out what the sweet spot is. Generally, I think it's a bad idea to raise too much money too early at too high a valuation. Instead, you want to raise money just for the next eighteen (or at minimum, twelve) months—enough capital to last you, ideally, a year and a half.

Of course, it depends on what type of business you're in, but the formula I recommend when you're going out to raise money is to **calculate your costs for the next eighteen months and then add 20–30 percent on top of that**. You need to have a buffer for the unexpected.

In stage financing, that money is the seed. But then, as you move through your cash cycle—when you have, say, nine months of cash left—you can go out and raise *more* money. Nine months in, hopefully you've proven certain aspects of your business;

you've been able to show that you can support growth and that your customer likes what you're selling (enjoying your product). You use those metrics to raise more money, but you *don't* wait until your cash runs out.

That's a much better approach, in my opinion, than raising a ton of money at a super high valuation from the start. When you go out of the gate like that, you have to show incredible growth. In essence, you're raising money on the prospect of what you're going to be building—and if you then underdeliver, you might have to do a "**down round**." That means raising money at a lower valuation than the valuation following your last round. It's not the end of the world, but a down round can be pretty challenging for an early-stage business because it signals that the company's momentum has slowed.

> A "down round" is when you have to raise money at a lower valuation than when you raised before—not a happy scenario for an early-stage business.

I'll give you another example. I have a new company I funded with some guys in Colombia, called Aptuno. It's an online real estate rental business. In trying to figure out how much money we needed to raise, we put together a spreadsheet laying out all the positions we wanted to hire for—we knew we needed *this* many engineers, product people, customer service people, and more—and the costs of those hires. We mapped out our initial needs and added 20–30 percent to have a little cushion. Our goal was to execute on our plan for twelve to eighteen months. But we knew that if we got really good traction in the first six to nine months, maybe we would go out and raise more based on our initial results. Especially if we knew we were going to need a little more time to execute on our plan, maybe we'd try to raise more capital to buy a little extra **runway.**

You always want to make sure you have at least twelve, and probably eighteen, months of runway. That's how you determine how much money you want to raise. In some cases—for example, if you're a very experienced entrepreneur or if the market's frothy—maybe you want to raise a little more. But the eighteen-month runway equation is a good general rule of thumb.

Finally, once you raise some money and have your runway, remember that the key word in "runway" is "run"—you've got to run *hard* to make it happen!

What you don't want, of course, is to run out of money. Founders are typically optimists, and so they often underestimate how much money they need and how long it will take to get to their next milestone. You always need to be asking yourself, what's the right balance? How can you ensure success and maximize the likelihood that you build something valuable?

Dilution is a sensitive subject for most founders, and even though an extra 1–2 percent dilution (or even 10 percent) doesn't make a huge difference, I've seen a lot of founders, particularly in Brazil and Latin America, who sell 50 percent of their business to early-stage investors. This is a huge mistake: it will instantly kill almost all future fundraising from venture investors.

Again, when it comes to valuation, just make sure you have a minimum of 12–18 months of capital, based on your costs. If you think you need $1 million USD, you should raise $1.5 million. You won't regret having a little extra cash: it will give you a helpful cushion for that extra hire or that unexpected pivot or problem that will likely surface.

Keep in mind that there are other specific factors that can affect valuation, too, like the strength of the market in a particular sector. For example, FinTech is hot right now in Latin America, and this is causing the valuations to go up. And it's just a strong economic climate overall: through 2019, it was really hot, particularly in Brazil, and so there were just bigger funding rounds than there had been in the past. Obviously this changed in 2020, but even post-COVID, there remains strong tailwinds in sectors of the economy that are benefitting from digitalization trends.

But the number one factor in valuation has always been—and still is—your growth.

PRE-MONEY VS. POST-MONEY

Entrepreneurs often get confused about valuation, which is why I thought it was important to give a basic explanation of how it all works, how valuation is determined. But as it relates to term sheets, one of the places where I see founders make a big rookie mistake—in terms of the economics of the deal—is in mistaking the "pre-money" valuation of their company with the "post-money" valuation.

Pre-money is the valuation of the company before the new investment is in. In other words, if the pre-money valuation of a company is $4 million and the investor is putting in $1 million, then the post-money valuation is $5 million—and you're selling 20 percent of the company.

Obviously, this distinction between pre- and post- has big financial implications and is an important thing to get clear on!

When an investor comes to you and says they'll invest $2.5 million at a $10 million valuation, there can be a massive difference in value (and dilution) depending on whether they mean pre- or post-money. But if the investor doesn't clarify and you're an inexperienced entrepreneur, you might think, "Oh, ten mil is great,"—not realizing the pre-money valuation is actually only $7.5 million.

Needless to say, there's a big difference between $2.5 million being invested at $10 million post-money or $12.5 million post-money. That's 5 percent of your company you're talking about!

> As a founder, you should always clarify whether the investor is talking about valuation pre- or post-money.

This becomes even more important when the initial negotiations happen verbally, as they usually do. You go in, make your pitch, present your deck: *This is our business, this is our team, etc.* Then, you say something like, "We're looking to raise two mil at an eight pre-money." (As founder, you usually don't come right out and say the value. Instead, you say something like "We're raising two million.")

You just have to always make sure that you're clarifying, especially when you're just giving these numbers verbally in your pitch and don't have a written valuation inside the deck itself.

Pre- and post-money is one of the most important concepts you need to understand when it comes to the economics portion of your term sheet. But there are a couple other relevant items here that we should go over as well.

EMPLOYEE OPTION POOLS

Having an employee pool is a massive factor in valuation. A lot of times, an early-stage investor will want to invest, say, $2 million at an $8 million valuation pre-money. That would put the business at $10 million post-money, with them buying 20 percent of the company. But the investor might also want you to create or expand your option pool. Why is this important to them? They're investing in the company and its future growth, and they know that in order for it to be as successful as they need it to be, the founders have to be able to attract really good talent. This is incredibly important: all the best companies are bringing great people. So, to make that happen, everyone has to give up a little of their equity to lure these great employees still to come.

When you're raising money from investors, they will want you to have an option pool—but they won't want you to create one *after* they invest. By definition, an option pool dilutes the equity of all the existing investors. Say the investor just bought 20 percent of your company, and you own 80 percent. Six months down the road, when you need to make some really important hires, and you are only now creating an option pool, using 10 percent of the company, that means now you own 72 percent, and the investor owns 18 percent.

Clearly, an investor like that would rather invest in a company that already had an option pool so that they would be able to keep their 20 percent share in the company and not see it diluted. This is why, when you're raising a round, most investors will want you to expand the option pool as part of the deal.

If you have one already or even if you are creating one and have leverage, then the size of the option pool and whether the new investors share in the dilution is negotiable. Maybe the investor will say they want a *bigger* option pool. Maybe you've only got 3 percent in the option pool. The investor might say, "You need a CTO; let's expand it to 10 percent. Your business really needs a CTO, and to get a good one, you may need to be prepared to give a full 5 percent of the company to them."

In talking about option pool, it's important here that we also discuss **vesting**. Typically, when you hire someone, there's vesting of the shares. We talked about this a bit in chapter three about co-founders, but it's also relevant for recruiting first-hires. Say you hire a really good employee and give them 1 percent of the company—but they only earn that 1 percent over time. Let's say it's a four-year vesting period with a one-year cliff (which is generally a good practice). The first year, they don't get anything. Then, once they hit the one-year mark (referred to as the **cliff**), it triggers a 25 percent option where they have the option now to buy. But they don't *have* to exercise the option. They can wait and do it whenever they leave the company. The rest of the shares will vest on a monthly basis (1/48 a month) over a three-year period.

The reason vesting is so important when recruiting executives is the same reason it's important when you're starting a company with a co-founder. The person may not work out! Say you hire a VP of engineering and give her 2 percent of the company, but then after six months, you realize you have to fire her. Because of the vesting structure, this person is not going to get any equity because they didn't complete their first-year "cliff."

But again, if the person makes it through the first year, they get their options, and then every month after that, they get 1/48 of the additional equity. After three years, they will have qualified for 75 percent of their equity. If they leave after three years, typically they have to exercise their shares and pay for them—but the shares are severely discounted.

At Viva Real, our option plan had a clause that whenever an employee left the company, they would have a three-month window to exercise their option. In retrospect, we probably should have made it a longer period of time. Three months made sense at first, but as a company grows, the **strike price** increases. A "strike price" means the amount of money needed to buy your option, and typically the value of the strike price is significantly less than the share price of the last round. (If you haven't raised capital, then the strike price will likely be a few pennies.)

But the main thing you need to understand is that vesting of shares is very common and it's something the investor may insist on and something that benefits the company as well. Same with employee option pools.

Finally, what are the economics if there is a liquidity event? In the term sheet, there is a term called **liquidation preference.** This means that the last money *in* usually has a "preference" (that's because the latest round is almost always the biggest) over the Common holders (founders and team) and often earlier investors. The way it works is that there's something called a *waterfall*: when a liquidity event happens and you pay out, the last investment that has the highest liquidation preference is the one who gets the money first. But if the company sells for a higher valuation than where the investor invested, then you clear the liquidation preference and it doesn't matter because everyone gets paid back their percentage ownership. Liquidation preference is really designed for downside protection for investors.

The investor will likely have many such requirements around the economics of the deal, as laid out in the term sheet, but beyond that they will also use various terms to establish a degree of *control*, as we'll see in the following section.

THE TERM SHEET: CONTROL

Who has control over the investment? How much ownership does the investor have? How much power does the investor have over the founder and the company?

There are a number of important terms on the term sheet having to do with control. A lot of this may be common knowledge to some readers, but in Latin America there is still a dearth of basic information like this—and that's what I aim to provide here.

First, there's what is called the **drag-along agreement**, which protects the investor in the event that the board of directors exerts the drag-along rights in their protective provisions. Say a shareholder wants to sell the company. If that person has drag-along rights, they can bring everyone into the sale. This can be a big problem if some people want to sell and others don't.

But if the *investor* has drag-along rights, it can be even more controversial. Maybe the founder doesn't want to sell, but the investor exerts their drag-along rights to drag all the other investors and say, "We're accepting this offer." That is why a lot of attention should be paid to how a drag along can be triggered and ensuring there is a balance between the rights of investors and founders/management (in the best-formulated contracts, both groups are needed to trigger a drag along).

> Drag-along rights give the investor very strong control over the direction of the company.

There are other important control factors as well. In fact, just having a board of directors is a big control factor.

As we talked about in Chapter Seven about boards, even board *observers* (who don't have voting rights) can be difficult. If you have several people with a bunch of opinions sitting on your board, it's not necessarily a control thing, at least not literally—but these observers can still have a lot of influence, for better or worse, on the decisions and direction of the company.

KNOWING WHAT MATTERS AND WHAT DOESN'T IN A TERM SHEET

Those are the two areas (economy and control) that investors will be spending the majority of their time on when they're putting together and negotiating the term sheet. Sure, some like to get deep into the nitty-gritty over all the different terms, but the biggies are really economy and control—and as a founder, these are the items you really need to think about.

It's very important for entrepreneurs to have this perspective on what matters and what doesn't. Less experienced entrepreneurs will grind and torture themselves over all the different terms—and not only is it a waste of time, but it distracts them from what they *should* be focusing on.

It certainly helps to have an experienced angel investor on board or a former founder who's seen a lot of term sheets—they know what is important and what is *not* worth freaking out about. In fact, often having that general help and advice is worth more to an early-stage business than having a lot of capital. It's also a good way to counter the **inherent advantage that VCs have over founders in these negotiations**. Think about it: for you, this is an infrequent transaction, but they've likely done it hundreds of times already.

It's the same reason divorce lawyers are so successful. When you get divorced, you think, *"Shit, I don't know what to do."* How would you? It's your first (or, well, maybe second or third) time going through it. But for the lawyer, they've seen it all before, again and again.

Same with a banker. They've seen so many deals. You haven't.

How do you get over this hurdle? How do you compensate for the fact that the investor is so informed in term sheet negotiation, and you're not? Guidance from your angel investor is one thing, but you also need a law firm to help you structure the deal.

The problem is that a lot of founders make the mistake of using the VC's own law firm as *their* company counsel. That's no good: you need to have your own law firm that represents *you* and has your best interest at heart, not the investors'.

Unfortunately, it's often the same one law firm that handles everything in these deals (even though, as a legal matter, they may have only one client: the VC).

Look, it's not the end of the world if that happens. In fact, other problems can arise when you have two law firms involved. The lawyers wind up nitpicking over everything. You just have to try to be as practical as possible about it. But in general, I recommend using your own law firm.

The truth of the matter is that the biggest factor you're going to have in your favor (in addition to being well informed and well advised), and the best way to counter the VC's inherent advantage, is coming into the negotiation with a lot of leverage (interest from different investors). It means you can pretty much push back on almost anything you want.

When you have multiple parties competing for a deal, it's called "deal heat"—and that's how you get the best valuation.

DEAL HEAT AND FOMO

I remember one time at Viva Real when we had a hot deal, I did something that's not very typical but was bold and effective. It was a piece of advice I got from one of my board members, Greg Waldorf. In a typical term sheet negotiation, what happens is that the investor sends you the document with their terms, and you respond. But because this was such a competitive deal, and we wanted to make sure we got the terms we wanted, we had *our* attorney draft the term sheet instead. Then, we sent it to the investor and told them just to fill in the blanks where it asked about money.

I am sharing that story here with a strong word of caution: I wouldn't advise you to try it unless you have a *very* competitive deal. If you do, and if the investor is very excited about the deal, then it's not going to be a problem. It's not going to piss off the investor. But if you're not entirely sure, don't do it. You definitely risk coming across as arrogant. In essence, you're saying: "We're not negotiating; this is what the deal *is* going to look like, take it or leave it."

Of course, the investor may not follow your instructions and instead mark up your term sheet and do a new draft of terms they don't like. But if you have multiple VCs that really want to invest in you, you have the upper hand and can even play them off one another and increase the value. Again, that's called "deal heat" and it's great for founders. But even if you're lucky enough to be in that situation, you should still be careful about potentially losing an existing investor by driving too hard. Keep in mind there's also the risk of setting yourself up for failure in the next round by creating such high expectations and then not delivering on them.

And always remember that valuation is not everything. Yes, you want to try to maximize terms, but there are also circumstances where it's smart to cede this or that desired term so that you can go with a fund with a superior reputation and have a great long-term relationship. It also may be the case that what's *most* important—even more so than the fund itself—is landing a particular partner on your board. Truth is, you'll find some excellent partners in less well-known or reputable VCs and you'll also find mediocre partners in top-tier VCs. I always advise founders to try as hard as they can to get the General Partners, as opposed to the associates, to take the board seats. Because they are more senior, they typically bring more value. The only exception to that rule is if a General Partner is already on too many boards.

Again, in determining how aggressive you want to be in your dealings with VCs, it's instructive to remind yourself of *their* psychology and refer back to *their* financial model.

In particular, keep in mind that all investors are looking for a "fund maker," an investment that pays for their entire fund. For example, maybe they've got a $100 million fund and they buy 20 percent of your company. From there, you grow and grow, eventually turning $1 billion plus business. The investor ends up netting $200 million from their $2 million investment (they would likely need to deploy additional capital to maintain their 20 percent stake, but this is just for illustrative purposes). They first need to pay back the $100 million in capital raised, but they get to keep 20 percent of the remaining $100 million. That one investment paid for everything. They will likely have a few other wins, but the windfall comes from their 100X return.

This is what all VCs are looking for. Everyone's running around trying to chase those "fund making" investment opportunities. The mania feeds on itself and causes a serious degree of FOMO in the VC world.

You can use this FOMO to your advantage.

By the same token, you should *never* make the mistake of telling an investor that there's no competition to invest in your company.

The point is to play on their FOMO. You *want* them to think there's a lot of competition. And you want there to *be* lots of competition. It's good for you to have multiple investors at the table. It's how you can ensure you have the best economic terms and just the best general terms in the term sheet.

Having that leverage makes all the difference. But you don't want to fake interest. Investors have extremely good sense about this—and if they call your bluff, you will be in terrible shape.

It's a delicate dance. You want *them* to come to *you*. But that's not always possible.

HOW TO CONTACT AND TALK TO A VC

What I did was totally wrong; a disaster, in fact. I went to LinkedIn and just sent cold emails to GPs at different VCs. Don't. Do. That. It doesn't work, and it sends the message that you're a total rookie.

The best way to get introduced or connected to a VC, by far, is through an existing founder, someone they're already invested in, who has already created value for the fund. If you know the VC has invested in such-and-such company, and you are friends with the CEO, ask her to introduce you to one of the partners at the fund in question.

Better yet, maybe you're a former employee at one of the companies that the fund has invested in. Maybe you worked at a hot startup before launching your own business. Say you ran marketing at the startup, and then you saw a tangential opportunity that was different than what the startup was doing. Now, you've left the startup and feel like you don't have the same currency that came with working for them. Don't be so sure of that. Let's say you were employee #4 at the startup. That means you went through the whole scaling phase with them. Your experience is valuable and impressive. Ask the CEO of the startup to introduce you to one of the partners at the fund in question. It means a big deal to have the CEO vouch for you. You can imagine how many inbound decks VCs receive and have to review. Being recommended by a CEO is a way to, essentially, get them to pay more attention from the get-go.

When I got Greg Waldorf and Simon Baker on board, the reality was that I had no connections, didn't know *anyone*. The startup scene is a weird club. Sometimes, it seems like everyone went to either Harvard or Stanford. Ironically, I was actually *from* the Bay Area but didn't know anyone in the industry and couldn't crack it for the longest time.

What finally allowed me to break into those circles was when I was executing and actually building a business—and was able to get someone on the inside to vouch for me.

Intros are everything, and other good sources for introductions are angel investors. If you have an angel investor who is connected with a VC, that's a pretty damn good "in." Lawyers and accountants are okay for intros, but there's not nearly as much value there as with founders or existing investors.

Finally, keep in mind that once you make your pitch to an investor, if they then tell you the opportunity is not right for them, don't even bother asking them to introduce you to someone else, a different investor.

It may seem like a good idea, but it's not. There's zero value there (in fact, there's negative value). Why is it such a bad idea? The perception of the second investor will inevitably be, *well if this business is really so interesting, why didn't the first person invest?*

Along the same lines, make sure that when you're fundraising, you carry yourself in a way that's engaging. People do business with people they like. That's why charismatic founders are better at fundraising. You have to be able to *tell a story.*

Your presentation is important. Not all founders know how to build a seed deck. Thankfully, there is a Y Combinator template for fundraising—it's called a YC deck template—that explains everything and provides a structure and flow.

A bad seed deck means you don't raise the money you need! However, I like this tweet from the founder of AngelList, Naval Ravikant, and think it applies especially to seed rounds:

Naval @naval · Jan 20

Time spent honing the pitch is better spent working on the product.

Good investors use your pitch to size you up, not to understand or appreciate the business.

♡ 79   ↻ 536   ♡ 4.1k   ↥

In 2019 I had a bunch of entrepreneurs participate in a "startup battle," where we had eight companies to present to me and a panel of investors. I coached all the companies beforehand and asked them to use a standard format, which was the YC template. It was extremely helpful for them to have that.

But regardless of template or format, the way a founder should be thinking when making their pitch—as we've learned so far in this section of the book—is to put themselves in the VCs shoes.

I remember when Rich Barton—founder of Expedia, Zillow, and Glassdoor—said that VCs think about three things when considering investing in a startup. He used the analogy of fishing:

- The density or amount of fish in the lake (market size/opportunity): if there's not a lot of fish, obviously it's not an attractive place to go fishing.

- Who's fishing (the team)
- Who's fishing next to you (your competition)

Now that you understand the VC's motivations, how they think about things, you will be in a much better position when you go out and fundraise.

But you must never stop asking questions and trying to learn as much as you can. The more you can know about how VCs operate, the better prepared you will be when you approach investors.

But you will still need to watch out for common pitfalls, which we will explore in the following chapter.

CHAPTER ELEVEN

COMMON PITFALLS

In the final chapter, Brian looks at some of the most common pitfalls he sees with founders who are looking for venture capital. He advises readers to ask for references and treat the whole experience like it's not just the investor interviewing you, but you interviewing the investor. What you should be looking for is a personality match and a balance with the rest of your board. You need to ask yourself: has this investor been through storms before, and how have they acted during these tough times (not only the good times)? Common rookie mistakes that founders make include asking for an NDA (VCs don't sign NDAs), getting too fancy/creative with the format of their pitch (keep it simple!), and misleading investors about the competition (saying they have a term sheet when they don't!). Often, founders also make the mistake of emailing all their existing investors with a request for help but not being clear about who they're actually asking. There are also pitfalls around money, such as not timing your fundraising well or not doing the work to nail down a lead investor. In the final pages of the book, Brian shares one of the worst mistakes he made: using a holding company that resulted in the company being exposed to US taxes, despite their business having no operation in the States, an oversight that cost them somewhere around $100 million.

Throughout this book we've seen the important role that investors play in recruiting and opening doors to potential customers—as well as facilitating introductions to other *founders* with similar experiences (who may be ahead of you along the path).

Chances are your early-stage investors won't *always* play such an outsized role, however. When you get to a certain scale, they tend to become a little less relevant, their help a little less vital. Of course, there are exceptions to the rule: sometimes a really good investor can and will scale up her advice. But in most cases, founders start to outgrow their early-stage investors.

That's what happened with us. Thomas and I grew up a *lot*. Initially, we got our Series A investors from a local fund—the two top investors in Latin America—and **persuaded them to split the round**. This rarely happens; almost always, one will want to lead. Investors don't like to share because it means less equity for them. So it was a big win when we got the two local investors to split the round (and had the effect of boxing them out so neither would invest in a competitor).

But later on, we still had these early-stage investors on our board—and when we merged with our competitor, ZAP, we got "diluted down," meaning the early investors now had less equity.

In our case, this new shareholder we merged with turned out not to be very active and didn't have any leadership on the board. In retrospect, we probably should have brought in a later-stage investor to drive the ship and help push the management team. Admittedly, we just didn't have enough leadership on our board at the time.

Throughout, I have been lucky to work with the very best investors in the region. Not only were they extremely helpful to me but also very *active* during that time in their role as investors in my business. Although this is a chapter about pitfalls in fundraising—of which there are many—the truth is that having great investors like Kaszek and Monashees allowed me and Viva Real to avoid (or at least sidestep) many of the challenges described in the following pages.

§ What are the red flags to look out for in a VC?   §

Realistically, most founders trying to raise money and build a company won't have the luxury of *deciding* who they want to work with. Only the very hottest businesses will.

No matter what your circumstances may be, however, you should always know what to look for in a VC—and what are the problems to keep an eye out for.

CHOOSING THE RIGHT PARTNERS IN A FUND

In finding the right fund, what really matters in the end is not only the tier/reputation of the fund itself but, maybe even more so, the quality of the person you're going to be working with. After all, they could be sitting on your board for years to come!

How, then, can you know if your investor is a person of real character? By spending time getting to know them! You can also ask for references. Look at which companies the VC has invested in, then contact those founders and ask them, "Hey, what's this person like to work with?" Talk to the CEOs of companies in their portfolio that are considered "big hits," but remember that it's equally important to talk to the other founders in their portfolio to get the full picture.

Of course, I understand that most first-time founders are dying to just get *any* investor on board. They can't be too picky or aggressive, right? Well, yes and no. Even if it's not a particularly competitive situation, the founder must remember that it's not just the investor interviewing them—*they're interviewing the investor* as well—as the investment will bear a lot of resemblance to a marriage (in good times and bad).

Moreover, it's just a good look to ask questions and do your research. It shows investors that you're engaged and serious about the process. Yes, it's certainly easier to grill your VC with questions when you're in a competitive position with your fundraising. But no matter what your situation, you can still benefit from the way you position yourself in your communications with VCs. When you ask, "How big is your fund? How much dry powder do you have left in the fund? What's your thesis?" it sends a powerful message to the investors: *this person knows what they are doing.*

Pay attention to how the investors respond—not just in terms of the answers but the *way* they respond.

You have to possess a real self-awareness about who you work well with and who you don't. For example, some people really can't handle the fist-pounding type; they just know they won't mesh well with an investor who's angry and aggressive. Then again, some founders are the opposite: they know they're going to *need* a hands-on investor who will give them that extra push.

There's no right or wrong here. It's all just about having the self-awareness around your own working style and what dynamic suits you best in a founder/investor relationship.

Aggressive can be okay but watch out for those early-stage VCs who are very nitpicky about the terms in the term sheet and all the granular details of your business. If you see that behavior in a prospective investor, it should raise an eyebrow—no matter what your work style may be—because it's a predictor of how they're going to act as a board member and investor.

Simply put, it creates the wrong dynamic. The **investor should *want* to empower the founder**. Yes, they should express their opinion if they feel strongly about something. But they can't force anything on the entrepreneur.

Especially if you're an early-stage company and you've just got a basic product, and now an investor is trying to rigorously evaluate your business and grill you on all the details, my advice is to get the hell out of dodge! There's just no reason for them to perform that kind of due diligence around an early-stage company—and if they're already so difficult to work with, you know it's only going to get worse!

Again, a good investor will want to *empower* the founder, not control them. Similarly, a good investor won't tranche their investment in early-stage financings over many payments. When a pre-seed or seed deal is tied to future KPIs, that's a big red flag because it can misalign interests (the investor may be rooting against you to meet the KPIs to have more leverage in the relationship). If you're like many startups, you're still figuring out what you want to be when you grow up. If your investors determine a narrow path for you, you don't have the flexibility to pivot into new opportunities that you come across.

Hopefully, you'll see the writing on the wall before it's too late. But what do you do *after* you have investors and they start pushing you in a bad direction?

If an entrepreneur doesn't agree with something an existing investor wants, the investor really has to just let go and accept. Otherwise, it's going to create unnecessary conflict. This is just common sense. It's the same philosophy I bring to hiring: I want to give my people the autonomy and freedom to make their own decisions rather than telling them what to do. I know that I can't work well with an investor who tries to control or micromanage. (It's a little different with a later-stage investor like a growth equity investor. They are more hands-on with numbers and in general.)

> Has your investor been through storms before? How have they acted and carried themselves during these tough times (not only the good times)?

There's no getting around it: at some point, you'll find yourself going through turbulent times with your investors.

The going can and will get rough, and for better or worse, these are also the moments when you see your partners' true colors—which is why it's so important to pay attention *now* to find the right ones. This is also why you want investors who have seen it all before and will stand by you through the challenging periods.

But in order to make the most of your investors, you also need to always *ask* for what you want.

PITFALLS AROUND INTERACTIONS WITH POTENTIAL INVESTORS

There is a certain etiquette you should follow when it comes to potential investors. For example, I've seen founders make the rookie mistake of asking an investor to sign an NDA. Big no-no. **No one signs NDAs.** It will just make people think that you're either: a.) a total neophyte, or b.) up your own ass thinking no one has ever had the same idea before. Either way, investors don't have time for that shit. And you should really know better: *no one's* trying to copy or steal your business.

I'll say it again: VCs don't sign NDAs.

There are some really late-stage growth companies—raising hundreds of millions of dollars—for whom it makes sense to protect their proprietary IP with an NDA. But most of the time, it's totally inappropriate.

Along the same lines, you should **always keep your pitches simple.** This isn't the seventies or eighties; *no one* does business plans anymore. It's just not how startups work. The whole startup game is about iterating fast, testing, validating. I know for a fact that, as an investor now myself, if someone sends me a long-ass proposal, it goes straight into the garbage.

That may sound harsh, but I'm teaching you the tough lessons now so that you don't have to learn the hard way later. And you can still have an internal business plan if it helps you. It's just *not* a useful document for fundraising. Investors don't have time to read a bunch of blah blah. They want *what they want*: a clear, concise PowerPoint presentation, nothing less, nothing more. (Of course, if the investors dig your slides, they will likely take a deeper look into your company and will then want to see real numbers, business goals, and so on in later rounds.)

I suggest all founders use DocSend. Sometimes investors don't like this. They don't like it because it gives you data about whether they've actually read through your deck. It also gives info about what slides they spent more time on. This can help you revise your pitch and understand what's potentially important for an investor. Lastly, people often, without the permission of the founder, forward a deck to others when it should be kept confidential. Sharing through DocSend reduces the likelihood of this happening.

Just keep your pitch simple. You don't need to reinvent the wheel or get so creative with how you present your business. You just need, first of all, your hook. That's your *one paragraph* that perfectly describes your company. Take the time to get this right: you're going to be using it a lot, emailing it to people, etc. For example, when a friend introduces you to an investor, you will just give the friend your paragraph to send to the investor as a point of entry.

But then you'll also need a *one-pager*, a one-page document (it literally must fit on one page) that highlights the specific points about your business.

Every time you pitch to a VC, you're learning and getting better at it. You're listening to the investor, seeing what kinds of questions they ask, and anticipating how to respond. It's a cumulative experience and it helps you greatly in tightening up your pitch: each time you interact with a VC, you remember the patterns you've observed before and are able to adjust accordingly.

Of course, you still may get a no.

People have a tendency to get mad when an investor passes. Don't take it personally if they don't understand your business. The smartest thing you can do is just politely, cordially engage the investor around *why* they passed. The more information you can extract from them, the more you can use it to sharpen your next pitch.

> Don't get emotional if an investor says no. Just listen and be very rational about it. Try to garner as much feedback as possible so that you can adjust and update.

Last but not least, whatever you do, don't ever tell an investor you've got a term sheet if it's not true. This may seem obvious but trust me: it can be very tempting to mislead an investor to believe that you have a fish on the hook already. You know how the game works. You know how important it is to get investors competing with one another; you know that the hardest thing in the VC world, especially in Latin America, is to get people to *move*; and you know, ultimately, that what *does* get investors to move, more than anything, is their FOMO.

Those truths are all completely legitimate, and the reality is that investors will indeed take their sweet time unless they think there is a danger of you closing with another investor. All of which is to say, I get it: it's tempting to pretend you have an offer. But if you don't actually have a term sheet, you're making a big mistake by saying you do. It's a small, small world. The truth can easily be sniffed out and you'll lose all credibility. If someone calls your bluff, you're screwed.

To be clear: if you actually *do* have a term sheet, however, by all means, you should shop it!

A term sheet is not the same as a done deal. But if you have a signed term sheet, even though it's not legally binding, it signifies with high credibility that your deal is indeed getting funded. (Especially for earlier stage deals, there's a very low probability that a company with a signed term sheet will not get funded.)

So if you have a term sheet, tell people you have it! Just **don't tell them who the term sheet is from.** Even if they ask, you're under no obligation to reveal the source, and many term sheets have confidentiality provisions that prevent you from doing so. (Fortunately, most of the good investors don't collude. But it does happen.)

In the VC world, every investor has their archenemy, and you can use this to your advantage. By not telling them who the term sheet is from, you trigger their competitive juices. The offer may not be from their archenemy at all, but what's the harm in letting them believe it could be?

It's a great way of leveraging FOMO and using it to raise greater funds—you're going to need enough to last you!

PITFALLS AROUND MONEY

How, then, do you know when you have to go out and raise *more* money?

One of the biggest pitfalls around soliciting VC money is *not timing your fundraising well.* Say you're building a company and you've started to scale. You managed to raise some capital, but like most early-stage companies, are not profitable yet: your burn rate is $30,000 to $50,000 a month. Obviously, you don't want to wait until you've only got one month of capital left to go out and raise more money. You want to make sure you always give yourself at least twelve months of runway.

Again, this may seem obvious, but sometimes a founder will try to time the market or over-optimize and end up having to raise money at the last moment, in the clutch and in a way that feels desperate. Needless to say, it's a mistake to wait until then. **You always want to raise money when you don't *need* money.** You just make better decisions that way. And you're in a better position with investors.

Sometimes, you do have something instead where your existing investors do a bridge financing. This is called an *internal round* and I'm not crazy about the approach: yes, it's an option but keep in mind that no investor will do more than one bridge round. So if you go back to the same trough a second time, expect that to be your last opportunity to ask them for more capital (unless it is in a subsequent funding round led by an outside investor where they want to keep their pro rata).

Keep in mind too that an internal round is generally not a great sign to the market. When people notice that it's just your existing investors investing, it sends a subconscious message that you weren't able to raise money from other investors who provide stronger, independent validation of the business. Of course, there are exceptions to this rule. For example, if your business is growing like crazy and your existing investors preempt an investment because they just really want to put money in and increase their stake, obviously that's a good thing! You definitely want to position a bridge round this way with anyone external. Typically, however, most internal rounds/bridge financings are *not* seen in a positive light. The perception is that they reflect a company that could be struggling.

Another factor at play is that you always want your investors to take a **bite, not a nibble**. Perception matters here too: if it's well-known that a particular investor usually invests checks of $3–5 million and you get the same investor to come in really early but for less money, unfortunately, many times what people will think is, *why is that investor investing so little and are they unlikely to step up with a larger investment in the future?*

Bottom line: when it comes to soliciting and negotiating with VCs, do your homework. The extra time and energy now is more than worth it. For example, if you're not careful, you can end up, as a founder, wasting a lot of time pitching to random investors *who won't ever invest in you*—not because they don't like you but because, as a rule, they just don't invest in your sector. Going down this dead-end road can be a big-time suck.

Similarly, you need to have a plan about who you're going after as a *lead investor*. This is one of the big challenges when raising money. Say you're trying to raise $2 million. Even if you already have a bunch of people willing to each put in a $300,000 check, that money is unavailable to you if they all say their investment is contingent on a lead investor.

You've got to get someone off their ass to write that *first* check.

Many investors say flat-out that they just "follow" other investors. I can't stress this enough; it's how the VC world operates: you need that *lead investor* who defines or carves out the terms and is responsible for the lion's share of the round.

> Every time you raise, you need a lead investor. The same goes
> for an angel investor: if you're doing an angel round, there's
> got to be one angel who spearheads it.

Finally, don't make the mistake of trying to cut corners or cut costs when it comes to your lawyers. I learned this the hard way with a lawyer who was helping us set up our company. He was very US-centric and had never done this before with a startup like ours, i.e., focused on markets outside the United States. He had me create a Delaware C-Corp, which resulted in us being exposed to US taxes, despite our business having no operations in the US.

This was a small and ridiculous oversight, but it ended up costing us somewhere in the magnitude of $100 million in company value. Worst of all, this headache could have easily been avoided. We had a lot of unnecessary tension in the negotiation to merge and sell our company simply because I didn't have the right legal support. As part of my next venture, Latitud, we are going to help entrepreneurs avoid these types of mistakes as well as streamline the capital-raising process. To better understand the corporate and legal structure for startups in Latin America, I suggest you listen to the interview with Dan Green, Partner of Gunderson Dettmer, on the Latitud Podcast (http://podcast. latitud.com/995722/3859934-how-to-structure-your-startup-for-international-investments-dan-green-gunderson-dettmer). They are a top-tier tech law firm with deep experience in Latin America. Dan Green and Brian Hutchings run their LatAm operations and have been great partners to me over the years.

Our Delaware C-Corp debacle is just one example of how things go wrong with the design or structure of the details when raising capital. Make sure you avoid all such traps in your term sheet and pay special attention to the 2X liquidation preference or ratchet. These terms are not market standard for most VC deals and if they are in your term sheet, I would strongly suggest that you push back. Good VCs don't need to play games with their term sheets to generate strong returns, and you want economics and governance that are aligned with your investors.

Not to freak you out, but I will say this: if you screw something up in the term sheet with your first capital, it sets the stage in a bad way for all future investments. So be careful! And by all means, don't skimp when it comes to finding a great lawyer: you want someone who's not just the best but specifically focused on *venture*.

Furthermore, when you're raising money and have a term sheet and are negotiating the docs, I strongly advise that you **cap your lawyer's fees.** Decide on a reasonable amount in advance with your lawyer. Also, sometimes you can get lawyers to defer your fees in the early stage of a company (and most lawyers will wait on payment until the closing of a round). They do this when they see you as a startup with a lot of potential. Law firms don't make their money from tiny companies just starting out. They want you to be big and successful because then you will be raising more money or getting acquired—and that is where they make most of their fees.

You've got to be incredibly savvy in these matters. Again, there's an inherent bias at play. All I can tell you is to educate yourself and learn from my mistakes. For example, there are people, scam artists basically, who'll pretend they're there to raise money for you—but will charge you money.

If you encounter one of these creatures, run for the hills.

Now, to be clear, if it's a situation where you have an angel investor investing and they ask for additional equity as an advisor, that's completely fine. They also might get carried interest on capital they syndicate to their network. That's pretty standard in the Valley. But if anyone says they're going to help you raise money but charge you up front or a cash finder's fee, it's your cue to put on the brakes. That's just not how things work in VCs (again, unless you are raising big institutional capital with an investment bank like Allen & Company—and even then, they will charge you a percentage of the deal once it closes).

⸾ Finder's fees don't exist in the early-stage VC world!　　⸾

Another big mistake I made in these negotiations was to not, earlier on, have had my employees sign a PIIA (proprietary information and inventions assignment agreement). A PIIA is a simple form and the idea is to protect the company against past and present employees claiming the IP belongs to *them*. For example, maybe there's an engineer who built something important to the business and now says he owns the concept. Proprietary information was a big issue, famously, with the Winklevoss twins around who claimed to own the idea for Facebook. Often, these issues come up with freelancers as well.

Point is: every single person who works on your project should sign a PIIA from the very beginning. Unfortunately, we didn't do that—so when we went out to raise money and were asked about it, our new investors made us go back and get everyone to sign before we could move forward.

It was a big pain trying to chase down all our former employees.

Ultimately, it worked out. All's well that ends well. But not if you raise too little money and don't have enough to execute.

PITFALLS OF RAISING TOO LITTLE (OR TOO MUCH)

With venture-backed companies, typically everything is tied to milestones. You do *this* to get to *this* to get to *that*. It's all very succession-oriented, step by step when you're building a company. You might raise a pre-seed just to get you proof of concept. Then, after that, you start getting some customer feedback. Finally, once you've actually reached the point of having paying customers, you go out to raise your Series A.

If you don't raise *enough* money, however, you're not going to be able to hit the milestones that enable you to keep going—and that's a big problem.

It's **much worse to raise not enough money than to raise too much money.**

Look, there are pitfalls around raising too much money too. One very real mistake I've seen founders make in Latin America is to sell way too much of their company when they start out—thereby rendering it uninvestable!

Taking the highest valuation can be a mistake in a number of ways, and you should always be wary of choosing a valuation over the actual value. But again, this pitfall (of raising too much) is not as serious as its opposite (raising too little). On the one hand, if you raise too much capital at too high a valuation just because the market is super frothy, and then you don't live up to those expectations…yeah, okay, it's bad, but at least you have more of a runway to figure things out.

The truth of the matter is that raising *too much money* is not a problem many entrepreneurs are going to be faced with. It's a proverbial "good problem to have."

But if you're *not* raising enough money, and don't have as much as you need to meet milestones, then you're going to have some real soul-searching to do.

At this point, you have two options: you can try to just grind it out (i.e., keep grinding away to get over the threshold) *or* it may be time for you to restructure, downsizing the operation or positioning yourself for "acquihire" (if you have a strong product and engineering team doing something that might be valuable for a larger company).

That was highlighted starkly by companies that found themselves in that position when the COVID pandemic occurred in 2020—those companies became "acquihire targets" by competitors that had previously (before the pandemic) raised ample capital and could take advantage of changed conditions to be the acquirers and accelerate growth.

CONCLUSION

You Are Next

There is a Japanese concept, which I absolutely love, called *ikigai*. The word doesn't have a direct English translation, but essentially it means "reason for being." The idea behind it is that in order to figure out your purpose in life, you have to ask yourself four questions: 1.) what do you love? 2.) what are you good at? 3.) what does the world need from you? and 4.) what can you get paid for?

As you can see in the image above, the place where "what you love" and "what you're good at" overlap is where you find your *passion*. Similarly, the area where "what you love" and "what the world needs" overlap represents your *mission*.

Then, in the two bottom sections of this model, the overlap between "what the world needs" and "what you can get paid for" is your *vocation*, whereas the overlap between "what you're good at" and "what you can get paid for" is your *profession*.

In the middle of these four elements is your sweet spot, your *ikigai*. It's the intersection of passion, mission, vocation, and profession.

I bring this up to return to an important idea that I introduced at the very beginning of the book: **building a business as one of the most powerful accelerators for personal growth.**

When it comes down to it, acceleration is what my book has been all about, on both a micro and macro level: how do you raise capital and accelerate the growth of the business you're building in Latin America but also how do you best navigate all the ups and downs, as an entrepreneur and human being, to not only survive but rocket ahead of your competitors?

⸸ The best businesses, in my opinion, strike the *Ikigai* balance ⸸

With my two co-founders, Yuri Danilchenko and Gina Gotthilf, we are building Latitud, a new platform to democratize access to everything a new, aspiring, or seasoned entrepreneur needs to succeed. Our new fellowship brings together the top entrepreneurial minds and most experienced tech operators across Latin America to learn from each other and obtain hands-on mentorship from top experts in the region and Silicon Valley. Like any startup, we are still in our early days, and I am sure that our vision will evolve as we talk to more founders and learn in the process. I am tremendously excited about Latitud, not least because I see it as a way for me to pay it forward. Again, as I talked about in the book's opening pages, I've always felt a major sense of gratitude for everything I've been able to achieve, and I continue to see this region as one of the most exciting ecosystems, a place where everything is coming together in an incredible way—a combination of extraordinary talent and massive opportunity.

Therefore, I feel strongly that it is my responsibility, as well as my desire, to elevate this ecosystem in every way I can. Maybe this is *my ikigai*: to give back, not just in the economic sense but also in supporting and believing in the region. When I get a WhatsApp message from a founder thanking me for helping them with their capital raising or advising them on a difficult topic, it feels amazing.

In general, the way I look at local ecosystems is that what makes them (and the people who find success within them) so amazing is not just the way that founders help one another but how they reinvest in and support the next generation.

To anyone reading this book, whether you're already very successful or just getting started, your time is now—*you* **are the next generation**. Let's build this together!

ACKNOWLEDGMENTS

A special thanks to my friends that gave me feedback as I was writing this book. Yuri Danilchenko, Gina Gotthilf, Thomas Floracks, Eduardo Marques, Brian Hutchings, Dan Green, Mom and Dad, Lucas Vargas, Gabriela Levy, Diego Simon, Cody Field, Ryan Delehanty and a special thanks to Mark Chait who helped me put my thoughts, words, and experiences into book form. I loved working with you on this project. Shout out to the entire Scribe team!

I also want to thank my investors, advisors, and friends that have supported me on this journey:

To my dad and James Gray for believing in me when nobody else would. To my Colombian family who took me in, fed me all the time, and was the cosigner on our first office because nobody would rent to me. Thomas Floracks for your friendship and partnership. Diego Simon for everything you did to make this a reality. Lucas Vargas for taking over so I could go back to the US and be with family. Simon Baker for the many trips to Sao Paulo filled with precious tactical advice and tough love. Greg Waldorf for taking me under your wing and being a true mentor and CEO coach. Micky Malka for dropping pearls of wisdom on me over almost a decade. Wences Casares for treating me like family when I showed up for dinner. Julio Vasconcellos for blazing the trail. Shaun Di Gregorio for hosting me in Kuala Lumpur and sharing your playbook. Kevin Efrusy for the sage advice, practical thinking, and life perspective. Ariel Poler for the early support. Alex Torrenegra and Tania Zapata for the close friendship and believing in me early on. Jeff and Karen Requarth for writing me a check at a time of great uncertainty. Adam Requarth for being the best brother possible and consistent supporter. Jeff Fluhr and Jeff Holmes for your early support. Chamath Palihapitiya for giving me an alternative perspective. Bedy Yang for being an early supporter. Gordy Rubenstein for getting me an early customer and being an early supporter. Pete Flint for huge inspiration, mentorship (and lunches when I was a broke founder). Larry Illg for the numerous chats over the years. Jose Marin and Fabrice Grinda for taking an early bet. Errol Damelin for cutting a check in a Sao Paulo taxi. Jonathan McNulty for the advice to our team. Jihan Bowes-Little for reconnecting and being part of the story.

Also, special thanks to Nico Szekasy for your calm demeanor and consistency as an investor and Hernan Kazah for always challenging me in a supportive way. Big thanks to Santiago, Nik, Andy, and the rest of the Kaszek team. Many thanks to Eric Acher and Fabio Igel for your huge support, from recruiting senior execs to finding me a nanny. Special thanks to Marcelo Lima and Carlo Dupuzzo and the entire Monashees team. Thank you Chris Hansen for your incredible support and friendship. When Santa Rosa was burning to the ground, you gave me a roof. Eduardo Marques for digging in with me many times on pretty much any topic imaginable. Thanks to everyone on the Valiant team for letting me crash your office and eat lunch and drink the best coffee in SF. Marc Stad and Eric Jones at Dragoneer for your support. Many thanks to Victor Hwang, Hans Swildens, and Ira Simkhovitch at Industry Ventures. Thanks Tom Brener at Quadrant. Thank you to Jeremy Phillips and Nimay Mehta from Spark and Lead Edge for backing me.

Last and definitely not least, I want to thank everyone who I had the pleasure of working with at Viva. I had the opportunity to work with so many talented people, way too many to be named here. If you are reading this and we worked together at some point during this wild ride, rest assured that I learned something from you. Thank you from the bottom of my heart for believing in what was once a dream and for participating in this incredible journey!

ABOUT THE AUTHOR

BRIAN REQUARTH is the Co-Founder and former CEO of Viva Real, a leading proptech business in Brazil. He merged the company with ZAP Imóveis (owned by Grupo Globo) and became the Chairman of Grupo ZAP, which sold to OLX Brasil for R$2.9 billion reais. Brian raised $74 million dollars in venture capital funding for Viva Real and now invests in the most promising tech companies in Brazil and Latin America as an angel investor. He is dedicated to empowering the next era of entrepreneurs in the region. His new company, Latitud, will transform the Latin American startup ecosystem, creating a software-powered community, local content, and a number of digital products to help more founders in the region build amazing companies and access capital to fund their ventures.